Sundays

Sundays

A cookbook.

Sophie Godwin

murdoch books

London | Sydney

Introduction

For as long as I can remember, Sunday has been my favourite day of the week. Life just seems to slow down slightly, which for a hyperactive, always-busy human like myself, is immensely welcome.

Yes, sometimes I might feel as if I'm slowly dying from the night before, yet even then, there's joy to be had in a day of binge-watching and eating copious carbs; especially if the weather is particularly abysmal.

At other times, Sunday is about sharing and feasting with friends, eating breakfast at any time of the day, or slow-cooking something magnificent. Or perhaps it's a bath and a big plate of greens that I'm after as I prepare to start a new week. And, of course, no Sunday would be complete without something sweet.

As each weekend requires something different, I've chosen to separate the recipes by Sunday occasions, so that you can cook and eat exactly what you fancy in that moment.

① Sunday Brunchin'

I personally HATE early mornings, so the freedom of eating breakfast at whatever time you want – and spending more time making it – is joyous to me. Brunch is way more than just eggs on toast, although that has its place, of course (see my recipe for Miso Brown Butter Scrambled Eggs on page 17), which is why this chapter includes next-level chipotle Breakfast Tacos (page 14) and Sriracha Corn Fritters (page 22) to start your day with a bang. If you're more of a sweet breakfast fan, my Banging Banana Bread with espresso butter (page 38) has your name written all over it.

② Sunday after a Big Saturday

Had a late night or a busy weekend? For those moments when you're in need of comfort and carbs, I've got you more than covered. Maybe you're craving a savoury snack, such as my Epic Sweet Potato Wedges covered in harissa honey butter (page 56), or some Cheesy Leeks on Toast (page 47)? Pasta is always going to hit the spot – you've got to try the Cumin Lamb Pappardelle (page 54), which comes in a rich, numbing, spicy umami sauce. Hungover? Make my speedy Smashed Burgers (page 68).

③ Sunday Slow

You couldn't have a book called *Sundays* without having some slow-cook recipes in there. The ones that tick over while you have a good potter/read your book/do whatever you like to do on a Sunday... This chapter has got some epic bangers, including an 'Nduja Parmigiana with a Shallot & Caper Salad (page 77), which is even better than it sounds, the most unctuous Lamb Neck & Olive Ragu (page 81), and the naughtiest Next-Level Dauphinois (page 82). What is it about slow-cooked meat that is so outrageously delicious?

④ Sunday Reset

These recipes are a bit of me: the speedy, easy, veg-packed meals that I return to time and time again. Perfect for those occasions when you need a bit of a solo recharge, each recipe in this chapter serves two (the idea being that you could happily cook for yourself and have a portion ready for Monday lunch if you so desired). Personal favourites include Peanut Butter Dal with Tomato Broccoli Tarka (page 126), Cheddar & Chilli Jam Crouton Salad (page 123) and Spiced Aubergine Rice Salad with a herby coconut green chilli dressing (page 117).

⑤ Sunday Feasts

This chapter was inspired by my work as a private chef, and it's the one I'm probably most excited about. Each feast serves six people and consists of three recipes. I've organised each one so that you can cook elements ahead of time to take away any stress. It's smart cooking that will make you feel like a boss, and enable you to blow your mates away with some banging food. There's a feast for every season, every dietary need, every mood.

⑥ Sunday Sweets

People who say they don't like dessert have got to be lying, right? When I started coming up with ideas for this book, these are the ones that evolved first. Who doesn't want a slice of the fudgiest Kinder Chocolate Cake (page 160) or the Miso Popcorn Cereal Squares (page 183) with their cup of tea? Or how about pushing the boat out, and having a full-on baking sesh with my Coffee, Tahini & Chocolate Profiteroles (page 187) or Key Lime Meringue Pie (page 178)?

⑦ Sunday Extras

This is my next-level section: the big flavour-hitters that mostly include chilli – what can I say? I love spice. These condiments (and my best homemade granola) take slightly more effort, but once made, they last for ages, and you'll be putting them on everything. For example, think the most addictive crispy chilli oil you've ever tried (page 192). I've also suggested other recipes throughout the book that they'll work great on, in case you need any ideas.

Key to dietaries

V = Vegetarian

VG = Vegan

DF = Dairy Free

GF = Gluten Free

A few notes for you

I've been a recipe writer and chef for over ten years, and having written twelve cookbooks for other people, what I've learned is the importance of flexibility. Sometimes, you just might not have a specific vinegar in the cupboard, and that's OK. So, where possible, I've included interchangeable ingredients that won't affect the taste.

This applies to fresh ingredients as well. For example, sometimes I just tell you to use the greens of your choice, rather than naming a specific type myself. I hope this gives you more freedom to alter recipes to include your favourite ingredients, helps you minimise waste by using up what's in your fridge, and saves you from having to go to the shops unnecessarily, especially on a Sunday.

Although I've included measurements for things like oil for frying, these are really just guidelines. If you're the kind of cook who prefers to slosh it in rather than get out the tablespoons, go for it!

Through years of cooking for large groups of people, I've learned how much you can make ahead of time (and how much easier that makes things!) so I've added lots of storage tips for recipes when I can.

Wherever possible, I've avoided using fancy equipment, and where I have, I've offered alternatives to make it accessible for everyone to recreate these recipes at home. I will caveat this by saying two desserts do suggest using a blowtorch, but fire is super fun...!

There may be a handful of ingredients you've not heard of before, such as urfa chilli paste or gochujang, but trust me: if you can source them, they are absolute flavour bombs that you'll use time and again. Other than that, everything should be possible to pick up at your local supermarket.

Around 70 per cent of the recipes in this book are vegetarian. As much as I love a slow-cooked lamb curry, veg will always have a special place in my heart. Vegetables are incredibly versatile flavour-sponges, way cheaper than meat and often more exciting.

This is the way that I cook at home, and I wanted this book to be accessible for everyone – the more people I can inspire to cook, the better. I honestly couldn't be more hyped to have written my first cookbook in my own name. Thank you from the bottom of my heart for buying it. I hope you love all the recipes as much as I do.

Sunday is the day for cooking and eating and feeling present – even if that's with a hangover.

Soph x

Sunday

Brunch-in'

Breakfast Tacos

Charred chipotle tomatoes, fried kale, pickled jalapeño salsa and crispy egg tacos. You may not find these in a taquería in Mexico, but they're about to become your new favourite meal.

Serves 4 | Takes 25 minutes | V/ can be DF/can be GF

120g (4¼oz) kale

400g (14oz) cherry tomatoes

3–4 teaspoons chipotle paste

juice of 1 lime

8 small corn or flour tortillas (use corn tortillas to make this gluten free)

3 tablespoons olive oil

8 medium eggs

2 spring onions (scallions)

150g (5½oz) natural yogurt (use plant-based yogurt to make this dairy free)

sea salt and freshly ground black pepper

FOR THE SALSA

2 spring onions (scallions)

6–8 pickled jalapeños, plus extra to serve

1 tablespoon pickling liquid (from the jalapeño jar)

large handful of coriander (cilantro)

1 small garlic clove (optional)

juice of 1 lime

3 tablespoons olive oil

1. To make the salsa, roughly chop the spring onions (both green and white parts). Put in a blender or small food processor, along with the pickled jalapeños, pickling liquid, most of the coriander (stalks and all), garlic (if using), lime juice and olive oil. Blitz to a smooth green salsa, season to taste and set aside.

2. Heat a large frying pan over a super-high heat. Add the kale, season, then dry-fry, stirring occasionally, for a few minutes until slightly wilted and charred in places. Tip into a large bowl, and put the pan back over the heat.

3. Place the whole cherry tomatoes into the hot pan. Dry-fry for 3–5 minutes, shaking the pan occasionally, until the tomatoes are blackened in places and on the verge of bursting. Now take the pan off the heat and add the chipotle paste and lime juice. Toss so that each tomato gets nicely coated in chipotle. Season, then scrape into the same bowl as the kale.

4. While the tomatoes are charring, toast the tortillas in a separate pan over a high heat, wrapping each one in a clean tea towel once toasted to keep warm.

5. Once the tomatoes and tortillas are cooked, put both pans back over a high heat and drizzle 1½ tablespoons olive oil into each. Crack in the eggs and fry to your liking. Meanwhile, finely slice the spring onions and roughly chop the remaining coriander.

6. Lay 2 tortillas on each plate. Spread each one with yogurt, then divide the chipotle cherry tomatoes and kale between each one. Top each with a fried egg, then spoon over the jalapeño salsa. Scatter over the spring onions and coriander, along with more pickled jalapeños if you like, for the ultimate Sunday win.

Miso Brown Butter Scrambled Eggs

I'm a bit obsessed with miso. Its super-savoury funk improves many things; it can be used to make a sticky glaze for veggies, or even swirled into caramel. Here, I've whisked it into eggs before cooking them in some butter that has been lightly browned (sounds fancy but is simple – I promise!) to create one of the most elite breakfasts around.

Serves 2
(easily doubled or halved)

Takes 15 minutes   V

4 medium eggs

1–2 tablespoons white miso
(depending on how funky
you like it)

1 tablespoon sesame seeds

1 teaspoon chilli flakes

2 spring onions (scallions)

handful of coriander (cilantro)

50g (1¾oz) salted butter,
plus extra for spreading

2 large slices of bread
(sourdough or crusty
white work well)

juice of ½ lime (optional)

sea salt and freshly ground
black pepper

1. Crack the eggs into a bowl or jug. Whisk with a fork until the whites and yolks are fully combined, then whisk in the miso until there are no obvious lumps of miso left. (The miso will act as your seasoning instead of salt.)
2. Toast the sesame seeds in a small, dry frying pan over a medium heat until lightly golden. Transfer into a small bowl and stir through the chilli flakes. Season and leave to cool.
3. Finely slice the spring onions (both green and white parts) and roughly chop the coriander (stalks and all).
4. Melt the butter in the same small frying pan over a medium heat (no need to wash it first). Once the butter has melted, continue to cook, swirling the pan occasionally, until it has browned in colour and begins to smell nutty.
5. Meanwhile, toast the bread.
6. Once the butter has browned, reduce the heat to low and pour in the miso eggs. Every 20 seconds or so, stir the eggs, moving your spoon through the entire pan until you end up with big pieces of silky scrambled egg. The key is to take the eggs off the heat while they are still a little runny so they don't overcook.
7. Divide the toast between two plates and butter each slice, then pile on the scrambled eggs. Top with the spring onions, coriander and chilli sesame seeds, then squeeze over the lime juice, if using, to serve.

Harissa Broccoli & Whipped Feta Toast

Whipped feta is one of those things that sounds impressive; in reality, it just involves blitzing feta with yogurt. The result is something so salty, creamy and satisfying, you'll be putting it on everything. Here, it is used as the base for harissa broccoli, jammy soft-boiled eggs and cumin-spiced nuts – Sunday sorted. This one's dedicated to my mate Matt, who is broccoli incarnate.

Serves 2   Takes 30 minutes   V

handful of nuts (any kind you want; I like almonds or hazelnuts)

2 teaspoons cumin seeds

200g (7oz) long-stem broccoli

2 medium eggs

100g (3½oz) feta

zest and juice of ½ lemon

4 tablespoons Greek or natural yogurt

4 slices of bread (I like sourdough)

1 tablespoon olive oil

1–2 tablespoons harissa (depending on how spicy you like it)

sea salt and freshly ground black pepper

1. Bring a medium-sized saucepan of salted water to the boil.
2. Meanwhile, roughly chop your nuts, then add to a dry frying pan, along with the cumin seeds. Toast over a medium heat until the nuts are lightly golden and the cumin smells amazing, then scrape out into a small bowl.
3. Drop the broccoli into the boiling water and cook for 3 minutes, then, using tongs, remove from the water and set aside, keeping the pan on the heat.
4. Now add the whole eggs to the water. Boil for 6 minutes. Set a timer – you want them to be jammy.
5. Meanwhile, crumble the feta into a small food processor, along with the lemon zest and yogurt. Blitz until smooth, then season with salt, pepper and lemon juice to taste.
6. Once the eggs are boiled, run under cold water until cool enough to handle, then peel.
7. Toast the bread.
8. Place the broccoli in the same frying pan you used to toast the nuts and drizzle with the olive oil. Place over a high heat and fry for 2 minutes or so until the broccoli is nicely heated through. Add the harissa and toss together, then take off the heat.
9. Divide the toast between two plates. Spread each slice with the whipped feta, then top with the harissa broccoli. Halve the eggs and place on top. Season and squeeze over a little more lemon juice, then scatter over the cumin-spiced nuts to serve.

Pimped-Up Avo Toast

There's a reason why avo toast remains a stalwart on all brunch menus, yet I always feel short-changed when it hasn't been treated with love – give me acid, give me salt. Here, there's plenty of both. Topped with a chipotle cherry tomato salsa, this is one breakfast you'll be making on repeat. Make sure to buy a nice, ripe, squidgy avo.

Serves 2 | Takes 20 minutes | V/VG/DF

1 large ripe avocado

juice of 1 lime

2 large slices of bread (sourdough or crusty white work well)

sea salt and freshly ground black pepper

FOR THE CHIPOTLE CHERRY TOMATO SALSA

2 spring onions (scallions)

150g (5½oz) cherry tomatoes

handful of coriander (cilantro)

1 roasted red pepper from a jar (optional but delicious)

2–3 teaspoons chipotle paste, or 1–2 teaspoons chipotle chilli flakes (if you can't get either of these, just use normal chilli flakes instead)

1 teaspoon ground cumin

½ teaspoon dried oregano

zest and juice of 1 lime

a good glug of olive oil (around 2 tablespoons)

1. Halve the avocado and scoop the flesh into a bowl. Squeeze in the lime juice, then mash together with a fork and season to taste.
2. To make the salsa, finely slice the spring onions (both green and white parts), quarter the cherry tomatoes, roughly chop the coriander (stalks and all) and chop the roasted red pepper, if using. Scrape everything into a bowl. Add the chipotle paste or chilli flakes, along with the cumin, oregano and lime zest and juice. Pour in the olive oil and season to taste.
3. Toast the bread and divide between two plates. Smoosh the mashed avocado over the toast, then top with the chipotle cherry tomato salsa and serve.

Asparagus Soldiers & Dippy Eggs

Asparagus, when in season, is one of the few vegetables I think tastes best flash-boiled rather than roasted, to retain its flavour. For me, nothing beats an asparagus spear dipped into a creamy soft-boiled egg and topped with parmesan, balsamic, capers, chilli – you know, all the good stuff.

Serves 2 | Takes 10 minutes | can be V (if using alternative cheese) / GF

250g (9oz) asparagus spears

4 medium eggs

1 tablespoon olive oil

1–2 tablespoons balsamic vinegar

20g (¾oz) parmesan, or vegetarian alternative, finely grated

2 tablespoons capers

big pinch of chilli flakes

sea salt and freshly ground black pepper

1. Put a medium saucepan of salted water on to boil. Put a frying pan next to it on the stove, but off the heat.
2. Meanwhile, snap or trim the ends off your asparagus.
3. Once the water is boiling, drop in the asparagus. Cook for 1–2 minutes until vivid green and just tender – I always cut a little bit off the end of one spear to check if it's ready. Remove with a slotted spoon and transfer to the frying pan.
4. Keeping the water on the heat, add the whole eggs. Boil for 4½ minutes (set a timer – you want them to be good for dipping, so getting the timing right is essential).
5. Once the eggs are about halfway through cooking, drizzle the asparagus with the olive oil, then season. Place the frying pan over a high heat and fry for 30 seconds or so to reheat.
6. Divide the asparagus between two plates. Slosh over the balsamic vinegar, finely grate the cheese over the top, then scatter over the capers and chilli flakes. Pop each egg into an egg cup or shot glass. Make sure you have some salt and black pepper handy, and get dipping.

Sriracha Corn Fritters

You can't go wrong with a good corn fritter, and these are pretty next level, even if I do say so myself. Spiced with sriracha and Cajun seasoning, then topped with quick-pickled onions, creamy avo and salty halloumi – what's not to love? Feeling extra hungry? Add a poached egg and/or some fried chorizo.

Serves 4   Takes 40 minutes   V

2 ripe avocados

juice of 1 lime

550g (1lb 4oz) halloumi

sea salt and freshly ground black pepper

FOR THE QUICK-PICKLED ONION

½ large red onion (use the rest in the corn fritters below)

juice of 1 lime

½ teaspoon Cajun seasoning

FOR THE CORN FRITTERS

½ large red onion

handful of coriander (cilantro)

340g (11¾oz) tin sweetcorn in water

50g (1¾oz) self-raising flour (or use plain/all-purpose flour with a big pinch of baking powder)

1 tablespoon Cajun seasoning

1–2 tablespoons sriracha (depending on how spicy you like it), plus extra to serve

2 tablespoons milk

2 medium eggs

2 tablespoons olive oil

1. Preheat your oven to 120°C/100°C fan/250°F/gas mark ½.
2. To make the quick-pickled onion, finely slice the red onion and place in a small bowl. Add the lime juice and Cajun seasoning and season with a big pinch of salt, then scrunch together with your hands – this will help the onion soften and quickly pickle. Set aside.
3. For the fritters, finely chop the red onion and coriander (stalks and all). Scrape into a large bowl. Drain the sweetcorn, then tip into the bowl. Add the flour, Cajun seasoning, sriracha, milk and plenty of salt and pepper. Crack in the eggs, then beat together to form your fritter batter.
4. Heat 1 tablespoon of the oil in a large non-stick frying pan over a medium–high heat. Using up half the batter, dollop in 6 fritters. Fry for 1–2 minutes on each side until cooked through and deeply golden. Transfer to a baking tray and repeat with the remaining oil and batter to make another 6 fritters.
5. Once all the fritters are fried, transfer the baking tray to the oven to keep warm.
6. Peel, de-stone and slice the avocados. Season well with salt and pepper and squeeze over the lime juice to stop them going brown. Slice the halloumi.
7. Return the empty frying pan to a medium–high heat. Lay in the halloumi slices and fry for 1–2 minutes on each side until evenly golden and crisp.
8. Divide the corn fritters between four plates. Serve with the sliced avo and halloumi, then drizzle over some more sriracha. Top with the pickled onions.

Greens on Toast

This is without a doubt my most-cooked 'recipe' in the book. I've put 'recipe' in quotations, because how you make your greens on toast is up to you. No two versions are the same – that's the beauty of it. Use up your left-over veg, add a s**t ton of flavour and say hello to the easiest, most satisfying meal, at any time of the day.

Serves 1	Takes 15 minutes	V/ can be VG/ can be DF

Fry around 250g (9oz) of greens in a good glug of olive oil until tender

Start with your more robust greens, chopped into bite-sized chunks:

- long-stem broccoli or normal broccoli
- green beans or any other type of bean
- courgette (zucchini)
- asparagus

Then add your leafier greens:

- spinach
- sliced spring cabbage
- kale
- sliced pak choi

If I'm honest, I just use whatever I have in the fridge!

Stir in some herbs and spices

Add 1 tablespoon herbs and spices, such as:

- turmeric + ground cumin + ground coriander
- smoked paprika + fennel seeds + chilli flakes
- turmeric + mustard seeds + cumin seeds
- smoked paprika + ground cumin + oregano

Or 1 tablespoon spice blend:

- garam masala
- Cajun seasoning
- fajita seasoning
- Lebanese seven spice
- ras el hanout

Or use 1 tablespoon paste:

- harissa
- chipotle
- pesto

Finish with a squeeze of acid

- lemon
- lime
- any type of vinegar

Pile onto 2 slices of toast

Choose your favourite – I like sourdough, which I keep sliced in the freezer. Spread with butter, yogurt, cream cheese, tahini or peanut butter.

Top with some sustenance

Greens are destined for a creamy topper.

Eggs are always great:

- 1 jammy egg (boil for 6½ minutes, then run under cold water and peel)
- 1 fried egg (fry in the same pan you cook your greens in; just scrape the greens to one side of the pan and crack in the egg)

Or some dairy:

- 50g (1¾oz) crumbled feta
- 100g (3½oz) sliced halloumi (fry in the same pan you cook your greens in; just scrape the greens to one side of the pan to make space)
- 2 tablespoons Greek or natural yogurt

Or, if keeping dairy free:

- 100g (3½oz) cubed tofu (fry until crisp)

Then sprinkle over a topping

It's all about that crunchy, spicy, salty or herby element. I'd even double up here on a couple of your favourites.

Crunchy:

- toasted seeds
- dukkah
- salted nuts (I love cashews or peanuts)

Salty:

- capers
- cornichons
- chopped olives

Spicy:

- Crispy Bits Chilli Oil (page 192)
- Salsa Macha (page 193)
- hot sauce

Optional extras:

- chuck in anything else you want, such as chopped herbs from the fridge

Brunch/Best meal at any time of the day – sorted!

Greens on Toast

↓

page 24

Sausage Sarnie with Scotch Bonnet Ketchup

Sausage sarnies will forever remind me of being a hungover teenager, and Keith Francis, my best mate Haz's dad, enticing us out of bed by shouting: 'Sausage sandwiches are ready, girls!' This sandwich features an elite ketchup and slow-cooked caramelised onions for the ultimate sarnie.

Serves 4 | **Takes 1 hour 10 minutes** | can be DF

3 large onions

2 tablespoons olive oil

4 fat garlic cloves

thumb-sized piece of fresh ginger

1 teaspoon ground allspice (optional)

handful of thyme

400g (14oz) cherry tomatoes

75g (2¾oz) soft brown sugar

75ml (2½fl oz) apple cider vinegar or red wine vinegar

1–2 Scotch bonnets (I love using 2 here; you choose depending on spice preference and individual chilli heat!)

8 fat, good-quality sausages (I love pork, but you do you)

salted butter, for spreading (optional; leave this out to make it dairy free)

8 slices of bread (you choose – I like a nice, chewy loaf, such as a bloomer, seeded or sourdough)

4 large handfuls of rocket (arugula) or watercress

sea salt and freshly ground black pepper

1. Finely slice 2½ of the onions and scrape them into a saucepan over a medium–high heat. Pour in 250ml (9fl oz) water, then add a big pinch of salt. Cook, stirring occasionally, for 15 minutes until the water has evaporated.

2. Meanwhile, finely chop the remaining ½ onion. Pour 1 tablespoon of the olive oil into a frying pan over a medium–high heat. Add the finely chopped onion, along with a pinch of salt. Cook for 6–8 minutes, stirring regularly until golden.

3. While the onions cook, finely chop the garlic and ginger.

4. Add the garlic and ginger to the finely chopped onion. Cook for 1 minute more, then add the allspice, if using, followed by the thyme sprigs, cherry tomatoes and a big splash of water. Increase the heat to high and bubble away for 10 minutes until the tomatoes begin to burst.

5. Come back to the sliced onions; pour in the remaining 1 tablespoon olive oil. Cook over a medium heat, stirring regularly, for 15 minutes, until golden and caramelised, then take off the heat.

6. Add the sugar and vinegar to the frying pan with the tomatoes, leave to bubble away for 2–3 minutes more, then tip the mixture into a bowl. Add the whole Scotch bonnet(s). Using a handheld blender, blitz until smooth.

7. Pour the mixture back into the same frying pan and bubble away on a low–medium heat until you have a thick ketchup; this will take around 5 minutes. Season to taste. (The cooled Scotch bonnet ketchup will keep in an airtight container for up to 2 weeks in the fridge.)

8. Cook the sausages to your liking.

9. Once cooked, reheat the onions. Butter your bread, if you like, then spread over a decent layer of ketchup. Assemble the sandwiches with your sausages, caramelised onions and salad leaves, and more ketchup if you like. Winner!

Spanakopita-Style Omelette

After a canapé event, I had some leftover spanakopita filling: the winning combination of spinach, feta, mixed herbs and loads of spices. The next morning, I chucked it inside an omelette, and this beauty was born. This recipe serves one, as making an omelette for yourself is a nice act of self-love.

Serves 1   Takes 15 minutes   V

2 handfuls of baby spinach

handful of mixed herbs
(I like parsley, dill and/or
basil – you do you)

50g (1¾oz) feta

1 teaspoon ground cumin

1 teaspoon ground coriander

big pinch of chilli flakes
(optional)

½ teaspoon sumac or zest
of ½ lemon

1 tablespoon pomegranate
molasses (if you can't get this,
use apple cider vinegar with
a squirt of honey instead)

3 medium eggs

knob of salted butter

sea salt and freshly ground
black pepper

1. Roughly chop the spinach, then scrape into a medium bowl. Finely chop the herbs (stalks and all), and add these to the bowl. Crumble in the feta, then add the cumin, coriander, chilli (if using), sumac or lemon zest and pomegranate molasses. Season well with salt and pepper and mix together.

2. Crack the eggs into a separate bowl or jug, and whisk well with a fork until the whites and yolks are fully combined. Season with salt and pepper.

3. Melt the butter in a large non-stick frying pan over a medium heat. Swirl so that it evenly coats the base of the pan, then evenly pour in the beaten eggs.

4. Leave to cook for about 30 seconds until the edges begin to set. Using a spatula, drag some of the outside cooked egg into the centre of the pan, letting some of the raw egg run to the outsides. Do this a couple of times until the egg is just set, then spoon the spinach filling onto one side of the omelette. Using a spatula, flip the empty half over the filling. Cook for 30 seconds more, then slide onto a plate. Heaven.

Cheesy Egg & Bacon Bap

You can't have a brunch section without having a bacon and egg bap. What makes this one elite is the unexpected contrast between the cheddar-and-chive scrambled egg, the salty bacon, the hot sauce and the ginger-and-rice-wine-vinegar pickled cucumbers.

Serves 2

Takes 20 minutes

4–6 back bacon rashers, depending on how hungry you are (smoked or unsmoked – your choice)

½ cucumber

small piece of fresh ginger (about the size of your little finger)

2 tablespoons rice wine vinegar

4 medium eggs

small handful of chives (optional but delicious)

50g (1¾oz) strong cheddar

2 rolls or baps (I like a sesame brioche)

big knob of salted butter, plus extra to serve

2 handfuls of spinach

hot sauce, to serve

sea salt and freshly ground black pepper

1. Cook the bacon to your liking (you can roast, grill or fry it).
2. Meanwhile, peel the cucumber into long ribbons down to the core (I then munch the core). Place in a bowl, then finely grate in the ginger. Add the rice wine vinegar and a good pinch of salt. Set aside to quickly pickle.
3. Crack the eggs into another bowl or jug and whisk well with a fork until the whites and yolks are fully combined. Season well, then snip in your chives (if using) and finely grate in the cheese.
4. Heat a medium-sized frying pan over a medium–high heat. Cut your rolls in half, then lightly toast, cut-side down, in the dry pan. Remove and butter the bases while still warm. Alternatively, you can place them cut-side down in the bacon grease so the rolls soak it up; this is my fave way of doing it, but you do you!
5. Reduce the heat to low, and add the butter to the frying pan. Once melted, pour in the cheesy eggs. Every 20 seconds or so, stir the eggs, moving your spoon through the entire pan until you end up with big pieces of silky scrambled egg. The secret is to take the eggs off the heat while they are still a little runny, so they don't overcook.
6. Assembly time. Divide the spinach between the roll bases, then layer on the bacon and cheesy scrambled eggs. Top with the pickled cucumbers. Squeeze hot sauce onto the lids of the roll, then sandwich together to serve.

Salsa Macha Pan Con Tomate

When tomatoes are in season, you can't beat the simplicity of grated seasoned tomatoes on garlicky bread – the Spanish know where it's at. Here, I've dialled it up, adding some smoky, fruity spice by spooning over some salsa macha, the Mexican condiment, my recipe for which can be found in the Sunday Extras chapter on page 193. So good.

Serves 1 (easily doubled)   Takes less than 10 minutes   V/VG/DF

2 thick slices of bread
(I like ciabatta or sourdough)

2 super-ripe juicy tomatoes

½ small garlic clove

2 tablespoons Salsa Macha
(page 193)

sea salt and freshly ground
black pepper

1. Toast the bread.
2. Meanwhile, using the coarse side of a grater, grate the tomatoes into a wide, shallow bowl, discarding the skins. Season with sea salt and black pepper to taste.
3. Rub the garlic across both sides of the toast, then put the toast on a plate. Top with the seasoned tomatoes, then spoon over the salsa macha to serve.

Chilli Jam BLT Bagel

This is the ultimate hangover bagel, but it's also great for any time you need a salty, tangy, chilli-spiked hit. Which is pretty much always... Salt and vinegar crisps for brunch might sound unorthodox, but hey, it's a Sunday, right?

Serves 2   Takes 20 minutes   DF

6–8 streaky bacon rashers, depending on how hungry you are (smoked or unsmoked – your choice)

100g (3½oz) cherry tomatoes

1–2 tablespoons sherry vinegar or red wine vinegar

3 tablespoons chilli jam

2 tablespoons mayonnaise

½ Baby Gem lettuce (I like to use the outer leaves)

2 bagels (I love sesame, but you do you)

salt and vinegar crisps, to serve (optional, but an elite combination)

sea salt and freshly ground black pepper

1. Preheat your grill to high. Line a large roasting tray with foil, then lay your bacon rashers on top. Grill for 4–6 minutes, flipping halfway through, until the bacon is mostly crisp and golden.
2. Meanwhile, halve your cherry tomatoes. Put them into a bowl and season, then pour over the vinegar. In a separate small bowl, mix 1 tablespoon of the chilli jam with the mayonnaise. Separate your Baby Gem leaves.
3. Come back to the bacon. Brush the rashers with the remaining 2 tablespoons chilli jam and grill for a further minute or so until sticky and caramelised.
4. Halve and toast the bagels.
5. To serve, spoon the chilli jam mayonnaise across each bagel half, then layer up the lettuce and tomatoes on the bottom halves. Spoon over any vinegar from the tomatoes bowl, then top with the chilli jam bacon and each of the remaining bagel halves. Serve with salt and vinegar crisps if you want to make this seriously next level.

Banana Pancakes

Everyone loves a pancake for breakfast, and these tick all the right boxes; they're easy to make, fluffy and light, with the added bonus of being naturally sweet from the bananas. Every summer, I private chef for a wonderful family, and these are one of their most requested breakfasts. I hope you enjoy them too.

Makes 12 (Serves 3–4)   Takes 20 minutes   V/ can be GF

2 super-ripe bananas (the blacker the banana, the sweeter the pancake!)

3 medium eggs

½ teaspoon vanilla extract

1 teaspoon baking powder (use gluten-free baking powder to make it gluten free)

80g (2¾oz) plain (all-purpose) flour (use gluten-free flour to make it gluten free)

neutral oil (sunflower, light rapeseed or vegetable), for frying

your choice of toppings, to serve (such as yogurt, berries, maple syrup, chocolate spread)

sea salt

1. Break up the bananas in a bowl, then add the eggs, vanilla, baking powder and flour, along with a pinch of salt. Using a handheld blender, blitz into a smooth pancake batter.

2. Pour a drizzle of oil into a non-stick frying pan over a medium heat. Use a piece of paper towel to spread the oil across the pan evenly, then ladle three puddles of the batter into the pan.

3. Cook the pancakes for around 1 minute until the underside of each is cooked and bubbles appear on the surface, then flip and cook for a further 30 seconds on the other side.

4. Repeat the process, adding more oil if needed, until you have 12 pancakes. You can always keep them warm in a low oven while you cook the rest.

5. Serve the pancakes with your chosen toppings. Trust me, you'll be making these on a weekly basis.

**Almond
Croissants**

↑

page 39

**Banging
Banana Bread**

↑

page 38

Banging Banana Bread

I brought slices of this into work for breakfast, and one of my pals, James – a chef – said it was the best banana bread he'd ever had. Shout out to Milli Taylor for the ingenious technique of using demerara sugar to line the loaf tin and create an epic sugar crust.

Serves 8–10   Takes 1 hour 30 minutes   V

165g (5¾oz) salted butter

2 tablespoons demerara sugar

75g (2¾oz) pecans or walnuts

2 medium eggs

125g (4½oz) soft light brown sugar

3 ripe bananas (the riper the better here)

100g (3½oz) dark chocolate

150g (5½oz) self-raising flour

sea salt

FOR THE ESPRESSO BUTTER (optional but super delicious!)

½ tablespoon espresso powder (feel free to use decaf)

150g (5½oz) soft salted butter

1 teaspoon vanilla extract

3 tablespoons icing (confectioners') sugar

*
Tip: The banana bread will happily keep for up to a week at room temperature, well wrapped or in an airtight container. Keep the butter in the fridge, if not using the same day, and melt onto the toasted banana bread.

1. Preheat your oven to 180°C/160°C fan/350°F/gas mark 4. Grease a 900g (2lb) loaf tin with 15g (½oz) of the butter, then coat the base and sides with the demerara sugar.
2. Lightly toast the nuts in a dry frying pan over a medium heat for 2–3 minutes, then leave to cool. Melt the remaining 150g (5½oz) butter in a saucepan over a medium heat and leave to cool slightly.
3. Crack the eggs into a large bowl, then add the light brown sugar. With an electric whisk, whisk until the mixture has doubled in volume.
4. In a separate bowl, mash the bananas with a fork. Roughly chop the toasted nuts and dark chocolate and set aside.
5. Add the mashed bananas, melted butter and flour to the egg mixture, along with a pinch of salt. Briefly whisk until a smooth batter forms, then fold in the nuts and chocolate.
6. Spoon the batter into your prepared tin. Smooth out the top, then bake in the centre of the oven for 50–55 minutes until a skewer or a piece of spaghetti comes out clean. Leave to cool in the tin for 5–10 minutes, then transfer to a wire rack to cool completely.
7. Meanwhile, if making the espresso butter (which I highly recommend!), mix the espresso powder with 1 tablespoon boiling water in a large bowl. Add the butter, vanilla extract and icing sugar, and beat to combine – or, for an extra-luscious butter, use the electric whisk.
8. I like to serve this banana bread cut into thick slices, toasted briefly and then spread with the butter. You do you.

Almond Croissants

My last breakfast on Earth would be a black coffee and a still-warm almond croissant. Nothing beats the satisfaction of ripping off a bit, almond and sugar going everywhere, and dunking it into the coffee. So I thought, why not recreate the experience at home... Dreamy.

Makes 4

Takes 30 minutes

V

125g (4½oz) flaked almonds

75g (2¾oz) cold salted butter

75g (2¾oz) caster (superfine) sugar

½ teaspoon vanilla extract

1 medium egg

4 ready-made croissants

1 tablespoon icing (confectioners') sugar (optional but pretty)

sea salt

1. Preheat your oven to 180°C/160°C fan/350°F/gas mark 4. Line a baking tray with baking paper.
2. Toast 75g (2¾oz) of the flaked almonds in a small frying pan over a medium heat until lightly golden, then tip into a small food processor.
3. Cut the butter into cubes. Add this to the food processor, along with the caster sugar and vanilla, and a big pinch of salt. Crack in the egg, then blitz until you have a paste – this is your frangipane.
4. Using a serrated knife, cut the croissants in half and place on the lined tray.
5. Dollop a big spoonful of the frangipane into the centre of the base of each croissant and spread to fill, then sandwich the halves back together and spread the remaining frangipane across the top of each croissant. Scatter over the remaining (untoasted) almonds.
6. Bake the almond croissants for 12–15 minutes until they are a deep golden colour and the frangipane on top of each croissant has set. Leave to cool for about 5 minutes, if you have the patience, then dust over the icing sugar, if using, to serve.

Berry Crisp

Randomly, Pops and I ate a version of this when we chanced upon the kindest Airbnb host on the Scottish border, who made us this in the morning. Jammy berries cooked with a little lemon, with a buttery, oaty, cinnamon-and-brown-sugar topper. I mean, who doesn't want crumble for breakfast?!

Serves 3–4   Takes 40 minutes   V/ can be VG/ can be DF

400g (14oz) fresh or frozen berries (I like a mixture of raspberries, blackberries and/or blueberries)

zest and juice of ½ lemon

2 tablespoons plain (all-purpose) flour

2 tablespoons soft brown sugar

Greek yogurt, to serve (use plant-based yogurt to make it vegan/dairy free)

FOR THE CRUMBLE TOPPING

75g (2¾oz) plain (all-purpose) flour

25g (1oz) rolled oats

2 tablespoons soft brown sugar

½ teaspoon cinnamon (optional)

50g (1¾oz) cold salted butter (use plant-based butter to make it vegan/dairy free)

1. Preheat your oven to 180°C/160°C fan/350°F/gas mark 4.
2. Tip the berries into a large bowl. Add the lemon zest and juice, along with the flour and brown sugar, and toss so that they are evenly coated.
3. Tip the berries into a small baking dish – you want them to be in a compact layer.
4. To make the crumble topping, combine the flour, oats, brown sugar and cinnamon (if using) in the same bowl you used for the berries (no need to wash in between!).
5. Cut the butter into small cubes, and add to the bowl. Rub everything together with your fingers until you have a crumble-like consistency.
6. Scatter the crumble mixture over the top of the berries. Bake for 25–30 minutes until the top is golden and crisp and the berries are jammy and bubbling.
7. Leave to sit for a few minutes, then tuck in with a big dollop of yogurt. This is effectively crumble for breakfast, a major life win. Equally as delicious eaten cold the next day.

Sunday

② after a Big Saturday

Harissa Fennel Rigatoni

Harissa is my go-to spice paste for whenever I want a big hit of flavour with minimal effort, and it's especially good in pasta. I love fennel, but if you're someone who is usually put off by its strong flavour, try it here. Caramelised and soft, it adds texture and complexity to what is basically a very simple cherry tomato sauce.

Serves 2   Takes 30 minutes   V/ can be DF (if not using cheese)

30g (1oz) pumpkin seeds (pepitas)

1 large fennel bulb

200–250g (7–9oz) rigatoni or tortiglioni (depending on how hungry you are)

3 tablespoons olive oil, plus extra for drizzling

3 fat garlic cloves

250g (7–9oz) cherry tomatoes

handful of dill or parsley

1 lemon

2–3 tablespoons harissa (depending on how spicy you like it)

30g (1oz) parmesan, pecorino or veggie alternative (optional)

sea salt and freshly ground black pepper

1. Toast the pumpkin seeds in a small, dry frying pan over a medium heat until they start popping. Remove from the heat, sprinkle with salt and set aside.
2. Put a large saucepan of salted water on to boil. While the water is heating up, very finely slice the fennel bulb, picking off the green fronds for later.
3. Drop the pasta into the boiling water and cook for 1 minute less than the packet instructions.
4. Meanwhile, heat the olive oil in a large frying pan over a high heat. Add the sliced fennel, along with a pinch of salt, and fry, stirring occasionally, for around 5 minutes until the fennel is just softened and starting to caramelise.
5. Meanwhile, finely slice the garlic and cut the cherry tomatoes in half.
6. Add the garlic to the fennel and cook, stirring, for 1 minute more, then chuck in the cherry tomatoes, along with a ladleful of the water from the pasta pan. Bubble away, stirring occasionally, until the tomatoes have broken down into a sauce. Reduce the heat to super low.
7. Roughly chop the herbs and zest the lemon.
8. Once the pasta is cooked, drain it, reserving half a mug of pasta water. Tip the pasta into the sauce, then add the harissa. Stir to combine, then drizzle over a bit more olive oil and enough reserved pasta water, until each piece of pasta is coated in the glossy sauce.
9. Stir through most of the herbs and all the lemon zest. Season with salt, pepper and lemon juice to taste.
10. Divide between two bowls, then grate over the cheese, if using. Top with the toasted seeds, along with the remaining herbs and the fennel fronds, to serve. Banging.

Dad's Macaroni Cheese

I will always be nostalgic for my teenage Sundays: my stepmum, H, and I would curl up on the sofa, eating mountains of Dad's two-cheese, caramelised onion and bacon macaroni.

Serves 4–6

Takes 1 hour 15 minutes

1 large onion

8 back bacon rashers (smoked or unsmoked, your choice)

2 teaspoons olive oil

300g (10½oz) macaroni

150g (5½oz) extra-mature cheddar

100g (3½oz) Gruyère or Emmental

50g (1¾oz) salted butter

3 tablespoons plain (all-purpose) flour

600ml (21fl oz) milk

2 teaspoons English mustard

100g (3½oz) cherry tomatoes (optional but delicious)

Tabasco, to serve

sea salt and freshly ground black pepper

1. Preheat your oven to 200°C/180°C fan/400°F/gas mark 6.
2. Chop the onion, then add to a frying pan. Snip the bacon into the pan in small pieces. Add the oil, then cook over a high heat, stirring regularly, for around 8 minutes until the bacon is crisp and the onion is soft and golden. Take off the heat and set aside.
3. Meanwhile, put a large saucepan of salted water on to boil. Once boiling, drop in the macaroni and cook for 2 minutes less than the packet instructions, then drain.
4. Tip the cooked macaroni into a 20 × 30cm (8 × 12 inch) baking dish, then spoon over the cooked bacon and onions.
5. Grate the cheeses.
6. Melt the butter in a saucepan over a medium heat. Once melted, stir in the flour to form a paste. Cook the paste for 1 minute, then, bit by bit, pour in your milk, making sure to mix in the last bit before pouring in the next – this will ensure you get a smooth sauce. You can use a wooden spoon or whisk, whatever you find easier.
7. Once all the milk has been added, increase the heat to medium–high and bubble away for 3–5 minutes until nicely thickened – you want it to be the consistency of double cream. Add the mustard and three-quarters of the cheese. Stir until the cheese has melted, then season to taste.
8. Pour the cheese sauce over your macaroni, then, if using tomatoes, halve them and place on top. Finally, scatter over the remaining grated cheese.
9. Bake for 20–25 minutes until bubbling and golden. For a crispier top, slide under the grill for a final few minutes.
10. Leave to sit for a few minutes, then serve with Tabasco.

*

Tip: This can be made in advance: just assemble up to the point of baking, then cover and keep in the fridge for a day, or freeze for up to 3 months. If cooking from frozen, add an extra 15 minutes to the cooking time.

Veggie?
Swap the bacon for 200g (7oz) sliced mushrooms

Cheesy Leeks on Toast

I came up with this recipe one night after a catering job, when I was hungry and had some left-over cooked leeks. I toasted some bread, spread the leek on top, grated over lots of cheese, grilled it and sat with a glass of red wine, watching *Sex Education* and thinking, 'Absolute genius'.

Serves 1

Takes 30 minutes

can be V (if not using Worcestershire sauce)

1 leek, washed

1 tablespoon olive oil

big knob of salted butter, plus extra for spreading

2 garlic cloves

a few sprigs of thyme

1 teaspoon Dijon or wholegrain mustard

good slosh of Worcestershire sauce or a veggie alternative (optional but very tasty)

2 thick slices of crusty bread (I like a crusty white bloomer or sourdough – you can use sliced straight from the freezer)

50g (1¾oz) extra-mature cheddar, Gruyère or Comté (basically anything strong and salty)

sea salt and freshly ground black pepper

1. Halve the leek lengthways, then finely slice into half-moons.
2. Heat the olive oil in a frying pan over a medium heat. Add the butter and allow to melt, then chuck in the leek. Season, then cook, stirring occasionally, for 6–8 minutes until collapsed and softened.
3. Meanwhile, chop the garlic and pick the thyme leaves.
4. Add the garlic and thyme to the pan and cook for 1 minute more, then stir in the mustard. Season to taste, adding a slosh of Worcestershire sauce if using – I like to add loads of black pepper here – then take off the heat.
5. Preheat your grill to high. Place the slices of bread on a baking tray and lightly toast under the grill on both sides, then butter one side and pile the leek mixture on top.
6. Coarsely grate over your chosen cheese, then slide back under the grill until the cheese has melted and everything is bubbling and golden. Serve with some more Worcestershire sauce, if you like, and feel v. satisfied.

*
Tip: You can prepare the leek mixture a day or two ahead, or make a double batch and keep some ready to go in the fridge for all your carby snack needs.

Spicy Sausage Noodz

My first introduction to packet noodles was for breakfast the morning after Adam and I got engaged, and I realised I'd wasted many years not eating them. This is my tribute to everything I love about packet noodles: spicy, salty and warming you up from the inside.

Serves 2 | Takes 30 minutes | DF

3 fat garlic cloves

thumb-sized piece of fresh ginger

4 spring onions (scallions)

2 tablespoons rapeseed oil or other neutral oil

4 pork sausages

2 tablespoons gochujang

3 teaspoons cumin seeds

800ml (28fl oz) chicken stock

around 400g (14oz) veg (I like pak choi or Chinese cabbage, sugar snaps or mange tout/snow peas, plus something more robust like carrot or baby sweetcorn)

300g (10½oz) straight-to-wok noodles (egg or udon noodles are great)

juice of 1 lime

1 tablespoon soy sauce

2 tablespoons tahini or peanut butter

1. Finely grate the garlic and ginger. Cut 3 of the spring onions into 2.5cm (1 inch) pieces (green and white parts).
2. Heat 1 tablespoon of the oil in your largest saucepan over a medium–high heat. Squeeze the sausages from their skins directly into the pan. Fry for 5 minutes, breaking up the meat into small pieces with the back of your spoon until nicely browned. Stir in 1 tablespoon of the gochujang and 1 teaspoon of the cumin seeds. Fry for another minute or so until the sausage meat is crisp and a little caramelised, then tip out onto a plate.
3. Put the pan back over a medium heat. Drizzle in the remaining 1 tablespoon oil, then add the garlic, ginger, spring onion pieces and remaining cumin seeds. Cook, stirring, for 30 seconds more.
4. Pour in the chicken stock, then whisk in the remaining 1 tablespoon gochujang and bring to the boil.
5. Slice any more robust pieces of veg into bite-sized pieces.
6. Add your chosen veg to the broth and cook for 2 minutes, then drop in the noodles and cook for 2 minutes more.
7. While the noodles are cooking, finely slice the remaining spring onion (both green and white parts).
8. Squeeze the lime juice into the broth and season with the soy sauce.
9. Divide the noodles, veg and broth between two wide bowls. Drizzle over the tahini or peanut butter, then top with the crispy sausage and finely sliced spring onion, to serve.

Adam's Grandma-Style Pizza

Known as a 'grandma-style pizza' in the US, it relies on a baking tray and a home oven to get the crust super crisp. We've made the dough as easy as possible: just mix it together and let it do its thang.

Serves 3–4 (depending on hangover/hunger)

Takes 50 minutes, plus proving

can be V (depending on toppings)

---

salad, to serve (optional)

FOR THE DOUGH

½ teaspoon fast-action dried yeast

500g (1lb 2oz) strong white bread flour, plus extra for dusting

2 tablespoons extra virgin olive oil, plus extra for the bowl

2 teaspoons fine sea salt

FOR THE SAUCE

400g (14oz) tin chopped tomatoes (get the best quality you can afford; it will make all the difference to the flavour)

1 fat garlic clove

½ teaspoon dried oregano

large pinch of caster (superfine) sugar

1 teaspoon red wine vinegar

250g (9oz) mozzarella

50g (1¾oz) parmesan or veggie alternative

FOR THE TOPPINGS

It's up to you! Go classic with pepperoni, or go for anchovies, olives, peppers, red onion – whatever you fancy

1. Begin by making the dough. Put the yeast into a jug and measure in 325ml (11fl oz) warm water. Give it a good mix and leave for 5 minutes to rehydrate.
2. Tip the flour into the bowl of a stand mixer fitted with a dough hook, then add the yeasted water and olive oil. Mix on medium speed for 5 minutes until smooth and elastic. Alternatively, mix together in a bowl and knead by hand until you have a smooth dough with no lumps. Cover and leave for 30 minutes.
3. Add the salt to the dough, along with another 2 tablespoons warm water, and mix thoroughly until the salt is evenly combined. Cover and leave to prove for 3 hours until doubled in size and nice and puffy.
4. Get a roughly 20 × 30cm (8 × 12 inch) lipped baking tray and dust well with flour. Carefully scrape the dough onto the tray. Using floured hands, gently stretch the dough so it fills the tray. Cover and leave for another 2 hours to prove.
5. When the dough has 30 minutes left of proving time, preheat your oven to 220°C/200°C fan/425°F/gas mark 7 and put a thick baking sheet inside to get it nice and hot.
6. Meanwhile, make the sauce. Drain the tomatoes in a fine sieve, then tip into a bowl with plenty of salt and pepper. Add the garlic, dried oregano, sugar and vinegar, and use a handheld blender to whizz until smooth.
7. Spread the tomato sauce evenly across the top of the dough, leaving 2cm (¾ inch) around the edges for the crust. Tear over the mozzarella, then add the toppings of your choice. Grate over the parmesan, making sure to get plenty on the crust, where it will get nice and crispy.
8. Put the pizza into the oven, on top of the preheated baking sheet, and bake for 30 minutes until risen, golden and bubbling. Cut into 4 slices to serve. We like to eat this with a big ol' salad – you do you.

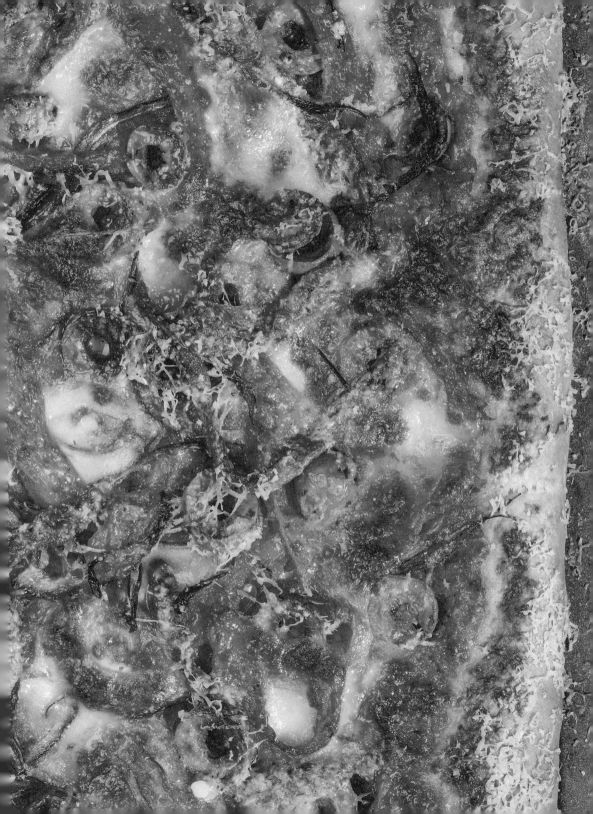

One Pan 'Nduja Orzo

This recipe came about when we had some left-over 'nduja and I wanted to make a quick, super-comforting one pot. The orzo cooks in the 'nduja and white wine sauce, while roasted peppers and spinach add a quick injection of veggies – plus there are salty capers and ricotta to give you that creamy hit. Parmesan-lover? Whack some on top, of course.

Serves 2

Takes 20 minutes

2–3 fat garlic cloves (you do you)

1 tablespoon olive oil

75–100g (2¾–3½oz) 'nduja (depending on how spicy you like it)

150g (5½oz) orzo

150ml (5fl oz) white wine

400ml (14fl oz) boiling water

2 roasted red peppers from a jar

2 large handfuls of spinach

2 tablespoons capers

zest and juice of ½ lemon

2 large spoonfuls of ricotta

30g (1oz) pine nuts, toasted

handful of basil

parmesan, to serve (optional)

sea salt and freshly ground black pepper

1. Finely chop the garlic cloves.
2. Heat the oil in a medium-sized saucepan over a medium heat. Add the 'nduja and cook until 'melted', using the back of your spoon to smoosh it into small pieces. Scrape in the garlic and cook, stirring, for 30 seconds more.
3. Tip in the orzo and stir so that each piece gets coated in the garlicky 'nduja oil, then pour in the white wine.
4. Once the wine has bubbled away by half, pour in the measured boiling water and season well, then leave to bubble away for 8–10 minutes until the orzo is just cooked, with a soupy sauce remaining.
5. Meanwhile, finely slice the red peppers. Add the peppers, spinach, capers and most of the lemon zest to the orzo. Stir until the spinach is wilted, then season with the lemon juice and salt and pepper to taste.
6. Divide the mixture between two bowls and top each one with a spoonful of ricotta, the remaining lemon zest, and the pine nuts, then tear over the basil leaves, to serve. If you are a parmesan fiend, grate some of that, too.

Cumin Lamb Pappardelle

This is a playful nod to Biang Biang noodles, originating from Shaanxi, China. Pappardelle is an amazing cheat's substitute for this spicy, numbing, crispy cumin lamb sauce.

Serves 4

Takes 35 minutes

1 tablespoon cumin seeds

2 teaspoons coriander seeds

2 teaspoons Sichuan peppercorns

400g (14oz) lamb mince

1½ tablespoons neutral oil (sunflower, vegetable or light rapeseed), plus extra if needed

4 fat garlic cloves

large thumb-sized piece of fresh ginger

3 tablespoons soy sauce

400g (14oz) pappardelle

a bunch of spring onions (scallions)

½ Chinese cabbage

50g (1¾oz) salted butter

1–2 tablespoons black rice vinegar, depending on how much you like it (if you can't find it, use balsamic vinegar instead)

4 teaspoons crispy chilli oil, plus extra to serve (make your own on page 192 or Lee Kum Kee is perfect here)

sea salt

1. Heat your largest frying pan or a wok over a medium heat. Add the cumin seeds, coriander seeds and Sichuan peppercorns. Toast until they smell amazing, then tip into a pestle and mortar.
2. Put the pan back over a high heat and add the lamb mince. Use your spoon to break up the mince into smaller pieces. Fry, stirring occasionally, for 8–10 minutes until browned and crisp. If it starts to stick, add a splash of neutral oil.
3. While the mince is browning, roughly crush the spices, along with a big pinch of salt. Get a large saucepan of salted water on to boil.
4. Come back to the mince. Reduce the heat to low and finely grate in the garlic and ginger. Add the crushed spices and 1 tablespoon of the soy sauce. Stir, cook for 30 seconds more, then scrape the lamb into a bowl. Take the pan or wok off the heat for a second, but don't clean it.
5. Drop the pappardelle into the saucepan of boiling water. Cook for 1 minute less than the packet instructions.
6. Chop the spring onions into roughly 5cm (2 inch) pieces (both green and white parts). Slice the cabbage in half lengthways, then chop into chunky pieces.
7. Return the frying pan or wok to a high heat – you want to get it searingly hot.
8. Once hot, pour in the oil, then add the spring onions and cabbage. Stir-fry for 3–4 minutes, until both are softened, then return the spiced mince to the pan. Mix everything together, then reduce the heat to low.
9. By now, your pasta should be cooked. Use tongs to transfer it to the frying pan or wok. Add the butter, vinegar and crispy chilli oil, along with the remaining 2 tablespoons soy sauce. Toss everything together so that each strand of pasta gets coated in the sauce.
10. Divide between four bowls, top with more crispy chilli oil, if you like, and ENJOY.

Epic Sweet Potato Wedges

A sweet potato, when roasted, is pure magic. Sweet, caramelised, crispy at the edges – it's pure carby heaven, especially when tossed with some spicy-sweet harissa butter. Game-changer.

Serves 4   Takes 40 minutes   V/ can be VG/GF

4 sweet potatoes

2 tablespoons olive oil

75g (2¾oz) super-soft salted butter (use plant-based butter if vegan)

2 tablespoons harissa

1 tablespoon honey, or maple syrup if vegan

2 tablespoons za'atar

sea salt and freshly ground black pepper

1. Preheat your oven to 220°C/200°C fan/425°F/gas mark 7.
2. Leaving their skins on, cut your sweet potatoes into wedges. Toss with the oil on your largest roasting tray. Season with plenty of salt and pepper, then spread into a single layer, making sure there is plenty of space between each wedge so they crisp up and roast evenly (you can use two trays if that's easier). Roast for 25 minutes, flipping halfway.
3. Meanwhile, in a small bowl, beat together the butter, harissa and honey. Season.
4. After 25 minutes, dot the harissa-honey butter over the sweet potato wedges. Return to the oven for another 3–5 minutes until the wedges are wonderfully caramelised and smell amazing.
5. Sprinkle over the za'atar to serve for the ultimate carby snack or side.

Anchovy Cabbage Spaghetti

Little beats a garlicky anchovy pasta. Here, I've made things more interesting by quick-pickling some shallot and sultanas for the ultimate salty, sweet, carby situ. Plus cabbage, because it works so well with spaghetti, and greens always make you feel better about life.

Serves 2

Takes 25 minutes

½ hispi/pointed cabbage

4 garlic cloves

200–250g (7–9oz) spaghetti (depending on how hungry you are)

1 banana shallot

3 tablespoons sultanas or raisins

2–3 tablespoons red wine vinegar or sherry vinegar

1 tablespoon olive oil

50g (1¾oz) tinned anchovies in oil

½–1 teaspoon chilli flakes (optional, depending on how spicy you like it)

large handful of parsley

50g (1¾oz) parmesan

sea salt and freshly ground black pepper

1. Put a large saucepan of salted water on to boil. Very finely slice the cabbage and the garlic cloves.
2. Drop the spaghetti into the boiling water and cook for 1 minute less than the packet instructions.
3. Meanwhile, finely chop the shallot. Scrape into a small bowl, then add the dried fruit and pour over the vinegar. Season and set aside to quickly pickle.
4. Heat the olive oil in a large frying pan over a medium–high heat. Add the anchovies, along with their oil, then stir in the garlic and chilli flakes, if using. Cook for 2–3 minutes, smooshing the anchovies with the back of your spoon, until they have broken down and the garlic has softened.
5. Chuck in the cabbage. Add a ladleful of pasta water, then stir and simmer away until the cabbage has wilted.
6. Meanwhile, roughly chop the parsley (stalks and all).
7. Once the spaghetti is cooked, use tongs to transfer it straight to the frying pan. Add the pickled shallot mix, along with the vinegar from the bowl. Stir through most of the parsley, then finely grate in half the cheese. Add another slosh of pasta water, then toss everything together until every strand of spaghetti is coated in a glossy sauce.
8. Season to taste, adding more vinegar if you like – and you'll want loads of black pepper – then divide between bowls. Top with the remaining parsley and grate over the remaining parmesan, to serve. Unreal.

Beetroot & Blue Cheese Baguettes

This is my go-to on-a-walk sandwich. It's unreal eaten at home, but even better when the beetroot has soaked into the baguette and you're starving mid-hike. I get it, it's way swankier than your average ham-and-cheese, but if there's one thing you should know about me, it's that I make a killer sandwich.

Serves 2 — Takes 10 minutes — V

1 chicory (witlof)

1–2 tablespoons balsamic or sherry vinegar (use a nice vinegar if you can)

olive oil, for drizzling

4 pre-cooked beetroots

100g (3½oz) blue cheese (I like a strong, crumbling Stilton here)

1 large baguette or 2 baguettines

2 tablespoons chilli jam (optional but very delicious!)

sea salt and freshly ground black pepper

1. Separate the outer chicory leaves, then finely slice the core. Put into a bowl and toss with the balsamic vinegar, a drizzle of olive oil to taste, and some seasoning.
2. Slice the beetroots and blue cheese. Halve the baguette or baguettines and drizzle the bottom halves with a little more olive oil, then spread over the chilli jam, if using. Layer in the beetroot and blue cheese, followed by the chicory and its dressing. Sandwich with the top halves of the baguettes.

Chorizo Chickpea Stew with Garlic Bread

I make a variation of this stew pretty much once a week. The combination of chickpeas, greens and sauce is a real winner. I love the smoky saltiness of chorizo here, but if you wanted to keep things veggie, you can sub it out for a heaped teaspoon of smoked paprika instead. And, of course, there's garlic bread – it's Sunday, after all.

Serves 3–4

Takes 45 minutes

1 chorizo ring (about 225g/8oz)

1 onion

2 red peppers

2 tablespoons olive oil

8 garlic cloves

handful of parsley

125g (4½oz) super-soft salted butter

1 small loaf of bread (tiger or bloomer work best here)

1 tablespoon fennel seeds

1 teaspoon chilli flakes

4 bay leaves (optional)

2 tablespoons tomato paste (concentrated purée)

250ml (9fl oz) white wine

2 × 400g (14oz) tins chickpeas (or a 660g/1lb 7oz jar – I love the Bold Bean brand)

600ml (21fl oz) chicken stock

200g (7oz) sliced kale or spinach

large handful of olives of your choice

sea salt and freshly ground black pepper

1. Preheat your oven to 180°C/160°C fan/350°F/gas mark 4 and line a roasting tray with foil.
2. Peel and slice the chorizo. Finely slice the onion and peppers.
3. Heat the olive oil in a large saucepan over a medium heat. Add the chorizo, onion and peppers and cook, stirring occasionally, for 8–10 minutes until the onion and peppers are soft and the chorizo has released all its oils and crisped up.
4. Meanwhile, finely grate the garlic cloves. Add half the grated garlic to a small bowl. Chop the parsley (stalks and all), and add this to the bowl too, along with the butter. Season well and beat to combine.
5. Using a bread knife, cut a deep criss-cross pattern across the top of the loaf of bread, making sure that your slashes reach halfway into the centre of the loaf.
6. Put the bread on the prepared roasting tray and stuff the garlic butter into the slashes. Bake for 20 minutes until oozing and golden brown.
7. While the garlic bread is baking, return to the stew. Stir in the remaining garlic, along with the fennel seeds, chilli flakes and bay leaves, if using. Cook for 30 seconds, then stir in the tomato paste and cook for 1 minute more. Pour in the white wine.
8. Once the wine has bubbled away by half, tip in the chickpeas, along with their liquid, then pour in the chicken stock. Bring the stew to a simmer and bubble away for 10 minutes, then stir in your greens.
9. Cook until the greens have wilted. Slice the olives and stir through, remove the bay leaves if needed, then season to taste.
10. Serve in the middle of the table with the herby garlic bread for people to help themselves.

'Nduja & Corn Risotto

Risotto is the ultimate Sunday food: a one-fork shoveller, comfort in a bowl. The combination of smoky spicy 'nduja and sweetcorn is next level. If you can't find 'nduja, this recipe would also work using a ring of chorizo cooked down until crisp with the onions, plus a big pinch of chilli flakes for added spice.

Serves 4   Takes 45 minutes   GF

1 large onion

1 tablespoon olive oil, plus extra to serve

4 fat garlic cloves

1.2–1.5 litres (40½–50¾fl oz) boiling chicken stock (a cube/pot or fresh works!)

100–150g (3½–5½oz) 'nduja (depending on how spicy you like it)

300g (10½oz) risotto rice (arborio or carnaroli work)

250ml (9fl oz) white wine

340g (11¾oz) tin of sweetcorn in water

large knob of salted butter

50g (1¾oz) parmesan, plus extra to serve

1–2 teaspoons sherry or red wine vinegar

handful of basil

sea salt and freshly ground black pepper

1. Finely chop the onion, then scrape into a large, high-sided frying pan over a medium heat, along with a pinch of salt. Add the olive oil and cook, stirring regularly, for 8–10 minutes until softened but not coloured.

2. Meanwhile, finely chop the garlic cloves. Make up your chicken stock.

3. Add the 'nduja to the pan with the onions. Use the back of your spoon to break up the 'nduja. Cook until it has 'melted' into the onions, then add the garlic and cook for 1 minute more.

4. Tip in the rice and stir so that every grain of rice gets coated in the onion mixture. Toast for a minute or so, then pour in the white wine.

5. Once the wine has been absorbed by the rice, add a ladleful of chicken stock. Cook, stirring regularly, until the stock has been absorbed, then repeat. Keep adding the stock in this manner until most of it has been absorbed and the rice is tender with a slight bite – this will take around 20–25 minutes.

6. Once the rice is tender, tip in the sweetcorn, along with its water. Melt in the butter and finely grate in the parmesan.

7. Give everything a good stir to combine. The risotto should be super glossy and unctuous with a loose consistency – add a little more of your stock if it needs it. Season with the vinegar, and salt and pepper to taste – I like a decent crack of black pepper here.

8. Divide the risotto between four bowls. Drizzle with a little extra olive oil, grate over some more parmesan and tear over the basil leaves, to serve. Sit on the sofa, watch some trash, feel restored.

Pork & Chive Dumplings

We've been eating a version of these dumplings in Chinatown for many years. Beijing-style, they couldn't be simpler: boiled and then served with a spicy, vinegary dipping sauce that, if you're anything like me, makes you feel alive. We like eating these with smacked cucumbers, like the ones served with the miso corn on page 70.

Serves 2
(or 3 if you're being polite)

Takes 45 minutes

DF

250g (9oz) pork mince
(use the best quality
you can)

handful of chives

thumb-sized piece
of fresh ginger

3 fat garlic cloves

2 teaspoons + 1 tablespoon
soy sauce

24 defrosted dumpling
skin wrappers

1–2 tablespoons black vinegar
(if you can't find this, use
balsamic vinegar instead)

1–3 teaspoons crispy chilli oil
(make your own on page 192 or
Lee Kum Kee is perfect here)

1. Put the pork mince into a bowl. Snip in most of the chives, finely grate in the ginger and garlic, then add the 2 teaspoons soy sauce. Give everything a good mix to combine the mince with the flavourings – I find using my hands is the easiest way.

2. Get a small bowl of water and place it close at hand, along with a large baking tray.

3. Spoon a teaspoon of the filling into the centre of a dumpling wrapper. Use your finger to wet the wrapper around the border, then gather it up around the filling to encase. Seal and twist; you should be left with a roughly round dumpling. Of course, if you fancy, you can fold it into a nice pleat – but I'm no good at that, so check YouTube. Place the dumpling on the baking tray, and repeat until all the wrappers and filling have been used up.

4. Fill your largest saucepan with salted water and put it on to boil. Meanwhile, mix the remaining 1 tablespoon soy sauce with the vinegar and crispy chilli oil in a small bowl to make your dipping sauce, adjusting the quantities to taste. I always like it super vinegary and spicy, but you do you!

5. Carefully lower the dumplings into the boiling water. Cook for 3–4 minutes until the wrappers are translucent and the filling is cooked through – I always check one before draining. Drain, then pile onto a plate.

6. Snip over the remaining chives and serve with the dipping sauce.

Roasted Cauliflower & Potato Curry

I love a vegan curry, especially one that is heavy on spice, giving you little pops of flavour as you're eating. To bring things up a notch, I've roasted the veg and added a crispy garlic-and-coriander-naan crouton situation. Banging.

Serves 4 | Takes 1 hour | V/ can be VG/ DF

500g (1lb 2oz) new potatoes

1 large cauliflower

6 tablespoons rapeseed or other neutral oil

3 tablespoons curry powder

1 onion

large thumb-sized piece of fresh ginger

1 green or red chilli

7 garlic cloves

handful of coriander (cilantro)

4 tablespoons whole spices (I like a mix of cumin, coriander, mustard and fennel seeds)

2 x 400g (14oz) tins coconut milk

100g (3½oz) baby spinach leaves

2 naans (check the ingredients if you're vegan)

juice of 1 lime

cooked rice, to serve

sea salt and freshly ground black pepper

1. Preheat your oven to 220°C/200°C fan/425°F/gas mark 7.
2. Leaving their skins on, slice the potatoes into 1cm (½ inch) rounds, then chop the cauliflower (stalk and all) into medium-sized pieces. Toss the potato and cauliflower on a large baking tray with 4 tablespoons of the oil and 2 tablespoons of the curry powder. Season, then spread into a single layer so they roast evenly. Roast for 25–30 minutes, tossing halfway.
3. Meanwhile, roughly chop the onion, ginger, chilli and 3 of the garlic cloves. Put into a blender or small food processor. Add the coriander stalks (keep the leaves for later), along with the remaining curry powder and 5 tablespoons water. Blitz to form a curry paste.
4. Heat 1 tablespoon of the oil in a large saucepan over a medium–high heat. Add the curry paste and cook, stirring regularly, for 5 minutes until the water has evaporated.
5. Add 2 tablespoons of the whole spices, cook for 1 minute more, then pour in the coconut milk. Quarter-fill one of the tins with water and pour into the pan. Bring to a boil, then reduce the heat to medium and leave the sauce to bubble away until the veg has finished roasting.
6. Add the roasted veg to the curry sauce and set aside the tray (don't wash it!). Stir carefully. Dump in the spinach, then leave over a low heat to wilt.
7. For the naan croutons, finely grate the remaining 4 garlic cloves into a bowl and stir in the remaining oil. Tear the naan into crouton-sized pieces, then place on the reserved tray in a single layer. Drizzle with the garlic oil and season. Roast for 5 minutes, then add the remaining whole spices, toss to coat and roast for another 2–3 minutes until the croutons are evenly golden and crisp.
8. Stir the lime juice into the curry and season to taste.
9. Top with the coriander leaves and garlic naan croutons. Serve with rice at the table. An epic win.

Chorizo XO Rice

XO is an iconic, super-savoury and f**king delicious condiment from Hong Kong, traditionally made using dried shrimps and scallops and a dry cured ham, *Jinhua*. Here, I've swapped the ham for chorizo and used shrimp paste, to give a big hit of easy, filthy flavour that will blow away any cobwebs. Think fried rice, but better.

Serves 2 | Takes 30 minutes | DF

½ chorizo ring

1 banana shallot

3 garlic cloves

thumb-sized piece of fresh ginger

1 tablespoon soft brown sugar

3 tablespoons soy sauce

2 tablespoons rice wine vinegar

125g (4½oz) basmati rice or a 250g (9oz) pre-cooked rice pouch

2 tablespoons neutral oil (sunflower, vegetable or light rapeseed)

1–2 teaspoons chilli flakes (depending on how spicy you like it)

2 teaspoons shrimp paste

200g (7oz) crunchy greens (green beans, mange tout/snow peas, sugar snap peas, asparagus)

100g (3½oz) soft greens (hispi/pointed cabbage, spring greens, pak choi, kale, spinach – that kind of vibe)

2 medium eggs

1. Peel and dice the chorizo. Finely chop the shallot, garlic and ginger. Mix the sugar, soy sauce and vinegar together in a small bowl, then set aside.
2. If using dried basmati rice, cook it according to the packet instructions.
3. Heat 1 tablespoon of the oil in a wok or large frying pan over a medium–high heat. Add the chorizo and fry for 5 minutes until crisp, then transfer to a bowl using a slotted spoon.
4. Add the shallot, garlic and ginger to the pan with the chorizo-infused oil. Reduce the heat to medium and cook for 5 minutes until the shallot is soft, then stir in the chilli flakes and shrimp paste. It will smell strong at this point, but don't worry – it will taste amazing!
5. Cut any larger pieces of green veg into bite-sized pieces, then add all the greens to the frying pan, along with the chorizo. Stir well so that everything gets coated in the aromatics. Cook for a couple of minutes, then push everything over to one side of the pan.
6. Pour the remaining 1 tablespoon oil into the empty half of the pan, then crack in the eggs. Cook the eggs, stirring, until scrambled, then mix them up with everything else.
7. Tip in the cooked rice (straight from the pouch if using pre-cooked), then pour in the vinegar mixture. Give everything a good stir to heat through, then divide between two bowls and serve.

Kinda Pasta
Alla Norma

The Italians know good pasta, and the Sicilian pasta alla norma – pasta with aubergine named after an Italian grandma – is one of my all-time favourites. For me, the beauty of pasta is that as long as you've got a good base, you can change it up depending on your mood, which is why I've included many delicious variations here, all of the salty variety, so you can really do justice to that craving.

Serves 4 | Takes 45 minutes | can be V

2 fat aubergines (eggplants)

2½ tablespoons olive oil, plus extra for drizzling

50g (1¾oz) tin anchovies in oil, or 100g (3½oz) 'nduja (both entirely optional but v. tasty)

4 fat garlic cloves

large handful of basil

1 teaspoon chilli flakes (omit if using 'nduja, otherwise it will be too spicy)

2 x 400g (14oz) tins plum tomatoes

1–2 tablespoons balsamic or red wine vinegar

400–500g (14oz–1lb 2oz) pasta of your choice (depending on how hungry you are)

2 handfuls of olives or 3 tablespoons capers (your choice of salty goodness)

50g (1¾oz) pecorino or parmesan or 125g (4½oz) burrata/buffalo mozzarella

sea salt and freshly ground black pepper

1. Cut the aubergines into medium-sized chunks. Season.
2. Place your largest high-sided frying pan over a high heat. Working in batches, dry-fry the aubergine chunks for around 4 minutes, turning halfway, until nicely charred on both sides. Tip into a bowl and repeat until all the aubergine is charred.
3. Drizzle the charred aubergine with 1½ tablespoons of the olive oil. This will give you a soft, smoky flavour later.
4. Place the pan back over a medium heat and add the remaining 1 tablespoon oil.
5. Add the anchovies or 'nduja to the pan, if using, and cook over a medium heat until 'melted', smooshing with the back of your spoon.
6. Finely chop the garlic and basil stalks, then add them to the pan, along with the chilli flakes, if using. Cook, stirring, for 1 minute, then tip in the plum tomatoes. Half-fill one of the tins with water and add that as well. Use the back of your spoon to break up the tomatoes, then add the vinegar and stir in the aubergine chunks.
7. Leave the sauce to bubble away for 20 minutes while you cook your pasta. Bring a large saucepan of salted water to the boil, then drop in the pasta and cook for 1 minute less than indicated on the packet instructions.
8. Stir the olives or capers into your sauce, season to taste.
9. Drain the pasta, then tip into the sauce. Tear in most of the basil leaves and toss to combine.
10. Divide the pasta between four bowls, then top with your choice of cheese. Drizzle with a little more olive oil and scatter over the remaining basil leaves, to serve.

Hungover Smashed Burgers

I love smashed burgers for two reasons. Firstly, the thin patties give you so much caramelisation, and because they are quick-cook, they're always juicy, never heavy or dried out. Secondly, they couldn't be easier; you don't even have to shape the patties beforehand. Taste-tested on a stonker of a hangover, Ad literally lost his mind for these. The combination of garlicky mayo, pickled jalapeños, cheesy burgers and CHILLI crisps is elite.

Serves 4

Takes 30 minutes

6 tablespoons mayonnaise

1 garlic clove

1 tablespoon pickled jalapeño liquid (plus the jalapeños, to serve)

2 vine tomatoes

¼ iceberg lettuce

100g (3½oz) extra-mature cheddar

4 brioche rolls

500g (1lb 2oz) beef mince (get the best quality you can afford; you want a nice high-fat content here. The meat makes the burger)

1 small pack Chilli Heatwave Doritos

sea salt and freshly ground black pepper

1. Spoon the mayo into a bowl. Finely grate in the garlic, then stir through the pickled jalapeño liquid. Season to taste, then set aside.
2. Cut the tomatoes into rounds and season. Finely slice the lettuce. Grate the cheddar. Cut the buns in half.
3. Heat two large frying pans over a high heat. Toast the buns, cut-side down, then set aside and let the pans continue to get searingly hot.
4. Divide the mince into 8 equal portions, but don't shape into burger patties.
5. Once the pans are super hot, take a portion of the meat and put into one of the pans, then immediately smash the mound of beef with a spatula or fish slice to flatten it into a gnarly burger patty. Repeat with all the meat, until you have 4 burgers in each pan, then season the tops of the burgers well with salt and pepper.
6. Fry for 2 minutes, not moving the patties, until the underside of each one has a beautifully browned crust. Now flip and season on the other side. Divide the grated cheese between the burgers. Cover the pans with lids (use baking sheets if they don't have lids), and continue to cook for a further few minutes until the cheese has melted. Take off the heat.
7. Spread mayo across the top and bottom of each burger bun, then layer the bottom buns with 2 burger patties each. Top with the tomatoes, lettuce, pickled jalapeños and chilli crisps, and finish with the burger bun tops. Be saved.

Miso Corn Rice

Miso aubergine has become a pretty iconic dish, and I wanted to riff on that using one of my favourite veggies, the corn on the cob. Trust me: when you take a bite of this buttery corn, you're going to lose your mind. For ultimate veggie pleasure, I'd recommend making your own crispy chilli oil (page 192). It's incredibly good – you'll be liberally spooning it on everything.

Serves 4   Takes 40 minutes   V/ can be VG/ can be GF

1 cucumber

300g (10½oz) basmati rice

4 corn cobs

50g (1¾oz) soft salted butter (use plant-based butter if vegan)

2 tablespoons miso

1 garlic clove

thumb-sized piece of fresh ginger

2–3 tablespoons rice vinegar

1 tablespoon Crispy Bits Chilli Oil (page 192) or 2 teaspoons of shop-bought crispy chilli oil, plus extra to serve

1 tablespoon sesame seeds

handful of coriander (cilantro)

splash of soy sauce (optional; leave this out to make it gluten free)

sea salt

1. Bring a large saucepan of salted water to the boil.
2. Meanwhile, using a rolling pin, whack your cucumber until it begins to break (v. satisfying), then cut into random pieces. Sprinkle with salt, then put into a sieve over a bowl or the sink and leave for 10 minutes so any excess liquid drains out.
3. Cook the rice according to the packet instructions.
4. If your corn are in their husks, unwrap them. Drop the corn cobs into the pan of boiling water. Boil for 5 minutes, then remove with tongs and set aside.
5. Melt the butter in a small bowl in the microwave or in a small pan over a medium heat, then beat in the miso.
6. Tip the cucumber pieces into a medium-sized bowl. Finely grate in the garlic and ginger, then add the vinegar and chilli oil, and toss to combine.
7. Place a frying pan over a high heat and add the corn cobs. Fry for a minute or so until beginning to char, then spoon all over with the butter and fry for a further 1–2 minutes until nicely coated and charred. Sprinkle over the sesame seeds and toss to coat. Transfer to a plate.
8. Roughly chop the coriander (stalks and all).
9. Divide the rice between four bowls and season with soy sauce, if you like. Pile on the smacked cucumbers and their dressing, then top with the miso corn on the cob. Sprinkle over the coriander and drizzle with more crispy chilli oil, to serve.

Curried Wings

Nothing beats a good chicken wing. Crispy exterior, tender meat and sticky sauce – it's got all the 'I've had a big Saturday' bases covered. In my version, the wings are cooked in curry powder, then glazed in a mango-chutney-and-hot-sauce combo for that sweet spice we all love. Plus there's a raita for dipping, and Bombay mix for added crunch, because why not?

Serves 2–4

Takes 1 hour

1kg (2lb 4oz) chicken wings (get the best quality you can afford – it will make all the difference to the flavour!)

2 tablespoons curry powder (mild, medium or hot – it's up to you!)

1 tablespoon baking powder

3 tablespoons mango chutney

3 tablespoons sriracha

2 large handfuls of Bombay mix

sea salt and freshly ground black pepper

FOR THE RAITA

¼ cucumber

small thumb-sized piece of fresh ginger

1 small garlic clove (optional)

handful of mint or coriander (cilantro) – your choice

150g (5½oz) natural yogurt

1. Preheat your oven to 200°C/180°C fan/400°F/gas mark 6.
2. Cut the wings in half at the joint, then pat dry with paper towels. Put them into a large bowl and season well with salt and pepper, then spoon in the curry powder and baking powder. Toss well so that each wing gets evenly coated in the curried mix.
3. Place two wire racks across two baking trays. Lay the wings across the racks – this cooking technique, plus the baking powder, are the secrets to getting the crispiest wings without frying them! If you don't have wire racks, you could use a grill rack instead.
4. Roast the wings in the oven for 40–45 minutes, turning halfway, until super tender, golden and crisp.
5. Meanwhile, make the raita. Finely chop the cucumber and add it to a bowl. Finely grate in the ginger (and garlic, if using). Chop the mint leaves or coriander and add these too, then stir in the yogurt. Season to taste.
6. Combine the mango chutney and sriracha in a saucepan, along with 3 tablespoons water. When the wings are cooked, tip them into a large bowl. Place the saucepan containing the mango-chutney mixture over a medium heat. Once bubbling, pour the mixture over the wings and toss to coat them in the sticky glaze.
7. Pile the wings onto a plate, then crush the Bombay mix with your hands, directly over the wings, sprinkling it all over them. Serve with the raita for dipping, a bowl for the bones and more paper towels – things will get messy, as they do with all the best food.

Sunday

③

Slow...

'Nduja Parmigiana
with Shallot & Caper Salad

① 'Nduja Parmigiana

Believe it or not, it's this recipe that got my publisher, Céline, excited about me. So, for that, and the fact that this is, hands down, one of the tastiest recipes I've ever written – thank you. It's your classic Parmigiana: layers of meltingly soft aubergine, rich tomato sauce and all the mozzarella, with a spicy porky twist.

Serves 4   Takes 1 hour 45 minutes   can be GF (check the 'nduja)

2 banana shallots

4 tablespoons olive oil, plus extra for drizzling

3 large or 4 small aubergines (eggplants)

100–125g (3½–4½oz) 'nduja (depending on how spicy you like it)

4 fat garlic cloves

large handful of basil

2 tablespoons tomato paste (concentrated purée)

2 x 400g (14oz) tins plum tomatoes

big pinch of caster (superfine) sugar (optional)

250g (9oz) buffalo mozzarella

50–75g (1¾–2¾oz) parmesan

sea salt and freshly ground black pepper

1. Preheat your oven to 200°C/180°C fan/400°F/gas mark 6.
2. Finely chop the shallots. Heat 1 tablespoon of the oil in a saucepan over a medium heat. Add the shallots and a pinch of salt. Cook, stirring occasionally, for 6–8 minutes until softened but not coloured.
3. Meanwhile slice the aubergines lengthways into long 5mm (¼ inch) slices. Put into a large bowl, sprinkle with salt and toss together.
4. Add the 'nduja to the shallots, using the back of your spoon to break it down. Once 'melted', finely chop the garlic cloves and finely slice the basil stalks. Add both to the pan and cook for 1 minute, then stir in the tomato paste and cook for 1 minute more.
5. Tip in the plum tomatoes. Half-fill one of the tins with water and add this too. Roughly break up the tomatoes with your spoon, then leave the sauce to slowly cook away for 30 minutes.
6. Meanwhile, pour away any liquid that has collected at the bottom of the aubergine bowl, then toss the aubergines with the remaining 3 tablespoons olive oil.
7. Heat a large frying pan over a high heat. Fry the aubergine slices in batches until golden and charred on both sides; this will take around 5 minutes for each batch. Transfer to a plate and continue until all the aubergine slices have been fried.
8. Returning to the sauce, season it to taste, adding a pinch of sugar if needed. Take off the heat. Pick the basil leaves.

$\longrightarrow$

Tip: The Parmigiana can be happily assembled the day before and kept in the fridge, then baked the next day.

↓

Veggie?
Leave out the 'nduja and sub for 1–2 teaspoons chilli flakes and 1 tablespoon balsamic vinegar instead, and sub the parmesan for a veggie alternative.

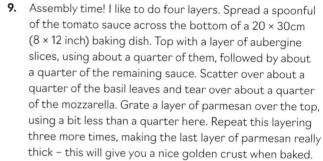

9. Assembly time! I like to do four layers. Spread a spoonful of the tomato sauce across the bottom of a 20 × 30cm (8 × 12 inch) baking dish. Top with a layer of aubergine slices, using about a quarter of them, followed by about a quarter of the remaining sauce. Scatter over about a quarter of the basil leaves and tear over about a quarter of the mozzarella. Grate a layer of parmesan over the top, using a bit less than a quarter here. Repeat this layering three more times, making the last layer of parmesan really thick – this will give you a nice golden crust when baked.

10. Drizzle with a little olive oil, then bake for 25–30 minutes until deeply golden and bubbling around the sides.

11. Leave to cool for 5 minutes (an unbearable wait) before digging in. Serve with the Shallot & Caper Salad (below). Mind-blowing.

② Shallot & Caper Salad

This tangy green salad with a mustardy caper, parsley and shallot dressing is exactly what you want to cut through the richness of our good-girl Parm above.

Serves 4   Takes 20 minutes   V/DF/GF

1 large banana shallot

2–3 teaspoons Dijon mustard

2–3 tablespoons white wine vinegar

5 tablespoons olive oil

3 tablespoons capers

handful of parsley

big pinch of caster (superfine) sugar (optional)

2 Baby Gem lettuces or 1 Cos lettuce

1 cucumber

sea salt and freshly ground black pepper

1. Very finely chop the shallot. Scrape into a salad bowl. Add the mustard, white wine vinegar and olive oil. Whisk together with a fork to create a dressing. Chop the capers and finely chop the parsley (stalks and all). Add these to the dressing, then stir and season to taste, adding a pinch of sugar if needed. You want the dressing to be quite tangy to cut through the richness of the Parmigiana.

2. Roughly tear the salad leaves. Chop the cucumber. Add these to the bowl with the dressing and toss to combine. Serve alongside the 'Nduja Parmigiana.

Sticky Beef Cheeks

I made up this recipe when one of my clients needed an impressive meal that was easy to reheat at home. The beef cheeks are braised until meltingly tender, then their cooking liquid is used to make a spicy, rich and fragrant sauce.

Serves 4–6   Takes 5 hours   DF/can be GF

800ml (28fl oz) hot beef or chicken stock

1.5kg (3lb 5oz) beef/ox cheeks

1 tablespoon rapeseed or other neutral oil

1 red onion

large thumb-sized piece of fresh ginger

4 fat garlic cloves

3 star anise

1 cinnamon stick

2 tablespoons soy sauce (use tamari to make it gluten free)

3 tablespoons sriracha

1 tablespoon caster (superfine) sugar

2 tablespoons rice wine vinegar

sea salt and freshly ground black pepper

TO SERVE
Pickled Chillies (page 196)

cooked rice

1. Preheat your oven to 160°C/140°C fan/325°F/gas mark 3. Take out a roasting tin that will happily fit the beef cheeks. Make up the stock.
2. Cut the beef into 5cm (2 inch) chunks. Season lightly with salt and pepper – you'll be adding soy sauce later, so you don't need very much.
3. Drizzle half the oil into a large frying pan over a medium–high heat. Add half the beef and fry for 5 minutes, turning regularly, until browned. Transfer to the roasting tin and repeat with the remaining beef and oil. Set the frying pan aside (you'll need it again later; no need to clean it).
4. Cut the onion into wedges, roughly slice the ginger and leave the garlic cloves whole, still in their skins. Arrange the onion, ginger and garlic cloves around the beef in the roasting tin. Add the star anise and cinnamon stick.
5. Return the frying pan to a medium–high heat and pour in the beef stock. Use your spoon to scrape off any of the beefy bits from the base of the pan, then pour it all into the roasting tin around the beef to mostly submerge.
6. Cover tightly in foil, then roast for 4–4½ hours until meltingly tender – the beef should fall apart when prodded with two forks.
7. Transfer the meat to a bowl and strain the sauce through a sieve into a medium saucepan. Smoosh the garlic into the strained sauce, then dispose of all the gubbins.
8. Add the soy sauce, sriracha, sugar and vinegar to the sauce. Cook until glossy and slightly thickened.
9. Meanwhile, shred the beef cheeks. Once the sauce is ready, add the meat and stir it through the sauce. It will look and smell outrageously good, and is ready to serve.

*
Tip: This can be made up to 2 days in advance and reheated. It also freezes super well; just add a splash of water when reheating from frozen.

Lamb Neck & Olive Ragu

I've been making a version of this for as long as I remember – the combo of tomato, olive and lamb bangs. Lamb neck, like shoulder, loves being slow-braised until it falls apart.

Serves 4   Takes 3 hours 15 minutes   can be DF/can be GF

500g (1lb 2oz) lamb neck

2 tablespoons olive oil

1 onion

2 carrots

1 small fennel bulb

4 fat garlic cloves

1 teaspoon chilli flakes

2 teaspoons fennel seeds

1 tablespoon dried oregano

handful of rosemary
or thyme sprigs

6 bay leaves (fresh or dried)

2 tablespoons tomato paste
(concentrated purée)

2 × 400g (14oz) tins
plum tomatoes

250ml (9fl oz) white wine

150g (5½oz) pitted green
olives (I like the queen olives
with lemon and herbs) –
I've also made this with
capers, if you prefer

1 lemon

sea salt and freshly ground
black pepper

TO SERVE
cooked pappardelle or
tagliatelle (see Tip if you want
to make this gluten free)

parmesan (optional)

1. Cut the lamb into 5cm (2 inch) chunks. Season liberally with salt and pepper.
2. Drizzle 1 tablespoon of the olive oil into your largest saucepan over a medium–high heat. Add the lamb and fry for 5 minutes, turning regularly until well browned. Turn off the heat, then transfer the lamb to a plate.
3. Finely chop the onion, peel and dice the carrots and dice the fennel. Scrape all the veg into the saucepan and add the remaining 1 tablespoon olive oil. Season with a big pinch of salt and cook over a medium heat, stirring occasionally, for 10 minutes until soft.
4. Meanwhile, finely chop the garlic cloves.
5. Add the garlic to the pan and cook for 30 seconds more, then add the chilli flakes, fennel seeds, oregano, rosemary or thyme sprigs and bay leaves. Stir in the tomato paste so that all the veg gets nicely coated, then tip the lamb back into the pan, along with any resting juices.
6. Add the tomatoes, followed by the white wine. Give everything a good stir, then cover with a lid and simmer away, still over a medium heat, for 2–2½ hours, stirring occasionally so it doesn't catch, until the lamb is completely tender – it should fall apart when prodded with two forks. (This can be done up to 2 days in advance and reheated – the flavour will only improve. It's also a great one for freezing – reheat with a splash of water, if so.)
7. Remove the bay leaves and rosemary, then shred the lamb in the ragu. Slice the olives and stir through, then season with lemon zest and juice, plus salt and pepper to taste.
8. I like to serve this tossed through pappardelle or tagliatelle, topped with loads of parmesan. YUM.

✱
Tip: For a gluten-free serving option, this is delicious served with crispy roast potatoes and a big slaw, such as the Pomegranate Slaw on page 111.

Next-Level Dauphinois

What could be better than dauphinois? Dauphinois with caramelised onions, garlic and thyme, PLUS anchovies and chilli – that's what. It's going to blow your mind.

Serves 6–8 | Takes 2 hours 30 minutes | can be V (cheddar version) /GF

3 large onions

1.5kg (3lb 5oz) potatoes (I like to use Maris Pipers or King Edwards)

50g (1¾oz) tin of anchovies, in oil

½–1 teaspoon chilli flakes

knob of soft salted butter

2–3 fat garlic cloves

50g (1¾oz) parmesan

handful of thyme sprigs

450ml (16fl oz) whole milk

450ml (16fl oz) double (heavy) cream

sea salt and freshly ground black pepper

Tip: I love making this in advance, baking it for 1 hour, then leaving to cool completely. To reheat, remove the foil and cook for 40 minutes.

↓

Veggie?
Omit the anchovies altogether, add 1 tablespoon of olive oil to the onions instead and swap the parmesan for 100g (3½oz) grated cheddar.

1. Finely slice the onions, then scrape into a saucepan over a medium–high heat. Pour in 250ml (9fl oz) water and add a big pinch of salt. Cook, stirring occasionally, for 15 minutes, until the water has evaporated.
2. Meanwhile, peel the potatoes and slice them very finely. Put the sliced potatoes into a large bowl of cold water – this stops them going brown and removes some of their starch.
3. Pour the oil from the anchovies into the pan and cook over a medium heat, stirring regularly, for 15 minutes, until golden and caramelised.
4. Add the anchovies and chilli flakes into the pan. Smoosh with the back of a spoon and cook for a few minutes until the anchovies have 'melted', then remove from the heat.
5. Preheat your oven to 180°C/160°C fan/350°F/gas mark 4. Rub the butter across the bottom of a medium-sized, deep rectangular baking dish.
6. Finely chop the garlic. Finely grate the parmesan. Strip the thyme from its sprigs into a jug, then measure in the milk and cream. Season generously.
7. Drain the potatoes from the cold water and pat dry with a clean tea towel. Now the assembly process can begin.
8. Fill the dish with a layer of potatoes, then top with some of the garlic, a little bit of cheese and some of the caramelised onions. Repeat until all the potatoes, onions and garlic have been used up, making sure to leave a good amount of cheese for scattering over the top. I never bother making the bottom layers neat, just the top one.
9. Pour over the cream mixture, pressing down the potatoes to make sure they are submerged, then scatter over the remaining cheese.
10. Cover with foil and bake for 1 hour, then remove the foil and bake for a further 30 minutes until the potatoes are completely soft (a cutlery knife should slide in easily) and the top is bubbling and golden. If you want a little more colour, slide under the grill for the final few minutes. Bliss.

Lamb, Coconut & Tomato Curry

The first home-cooked lamb curry that really blew me away was a Madhur Jaffrey recipe that included cardamom and cinnamon. There's something about these fragrant spices that goes so well with lamb. My recipe includes coconut milk for a creamy sauce and a kachumber-style salad to cut through the richness.

Serves 4　　　　Takes 2 hours 30 minutes　　　　DF/GF

500g (1lb 2oz) lamb neck

3 tablespoons vegetable or rapeseed oil

2 red onions

6 garlic cloves

large thumb-sized piece of fresh ginger

2 tablespoons whole spices (I like a mix of cumin, coriander and mustard seeds – use whatever you have)

2 cinnamon sticks

6 cardamom pods (optional but delicious)

2 teaspoons ground turmeric

2 teaspoons chilli powder (use hot or medium depending on how spicy you like it)

400g (14oz) tin plum tomatoes

400ml (14fl oz) tin coconut milk

cooked rice, to serve

sea salt and freshly ground black pepper

1. Cut the lamb into 2.5cm (1 inch) pieces. Season liberally with salt and pepper.
2. Heat ½ tablespoon of the oil in your largest saucepan over a medium–high heat. Add half the lamb and fry for 3–4 minutes, turning regularly, until browned. Transfer to a plate and repeat with another ½ tablespoon of oil and the remaining lamb. Turn off the heat.
3. Finely slice the red onions. Add the remaining 2 tablespoons oil to the saucepan, along with the onions and some salt. Fry over a medium heat, stirring occasionally, for 6–8 minutes until the onions are softened and starting to colour.
4. Meanwhile, finely grate the garlic and ginger. Add to the pan and cook, stirring, for 30 seconds more, then add the whole spices, cinnamon sticks, cardamom (if using), turmeric and chilli powder. Cook, stirring, for a further minute until everything smells amazing, then tip in the plum tomatoes and coconut milk. Half-fill the tin with water and add that too. Stir to combine and use the back of your spoon to break down the tomatoes a little.
5. Return the lamb to the pan, along with any juices. Give everything a good stir, then cover with a lid. Leave to simmer away over a low–medium heat for 45 minutes, then remove the lid and cook for a further 45 minutes–1 hour until the sauce has reduced and the lamb is completely tender; it should fall apart when prodded with two forks.

FOR THE KACHUMBER SALAD

1 red onion

4 vine tomatoes

1 cucumber

handful of coriander
(cilantro), and/or mint

zest and juice of 1 lemon

½ teaspoon chilli powder

6. Season the curry to taste, removing the cardamom pods and cinnamon sticks, if you like (I never usually bother, but you do you). Reduce the heat to low while you make the kachumber salad (now is also a good time to cook the rice).

7. To make the salad, very finely chop the red onion and scrape into a bowl. Chop the tomatoes and cucumber, and add these to the bowl too. Roughly chop the coriander (stalks and all), and pick the mint leaves, if using. Add to the bowl, along with the lemon zest and juice and chilli powder. Toss to combine, then season to taste.

8. Serve the curry with the kachumber salad and rice.

Tip: You can make the curry up to 2 days in advance and reheat it – the flavour will only improve. It's also a great one for freezing.

Chipotle Pork Shoulder with Slaw & Flatbreads

① Chipotle Pork Shoulder

The secret to this recipe is the marinade: you char the onions, tomatoes and garlic, and toast the dried chillies to add a smoky depth of flavour. It may seem an unnecessary step, but trust me, it's worth it – this recipe will have your mates wanting to buy the book. Plus, once the marinade is out of the way, it's just a case of letting the pork slow-cook and do its thing. Serve in flatbreads with the charred slaw on page 90.

Serves 6 | Takes 3 hours 30 minutes | DF

3–4 whole dried Mexican chillies (use whatever type you can get – I love chipotle, ancho or arbol here)

2 large red onions

1 garlic bulb

4 large vine tomatoes

1 tablespoon cumin seeds

2 teaspoons dried oregano

1 tablespoon smoked paprika

2–3 tablespoons chipotle paste (depending on how spicy you like it)

1.5–1.7kg (3lb 5oz–3lb 12oz) boneless pork shoulder

1 tablespoon olive oil

2 limes

1 orange

sea salt and freshly ground black pepper

1. Put the kettle on to boil and heat your largest saucepan over a high heat (this will be the same pan you'll cook your pork in).
2. Add the dried chillies to the pan. Dry-fry for a minute or so, turning with tongs until nicely toasted, then transfer the chillies to a jug and put the pan back over the heat.
3. Peel one of the red onions and cut it in half. Separate the garlic into cloves, leaving their skin on. Put the halved onion into the hot pan, cut-side down, along with the whole tomatoes and the garlic cloves. Dry-fry, turning occasionally, for around 5 minutes until everything is nicely blackened.
4. Meanwhile, pour 500ml (17fl oz) boiling water over the dried chillies and leave to soften.
5. Tip the charred veg into a bowl. Put the pan back on the stove, but turn off the heat. Add the cumin seeds to the pan and let them toast in the residual heat until they smell amazing. Tip them into the bowl with the garlic and tomatoes.
6. Peel the garlic cloves, then spoon everything into a blender. Remove the softened dried chillies from their soaking liquid (but keep the liquid; you'll need it later). Remove their stalks and add the chillies to the blender, followed by the oregano, smoked paprika and chipotle paste. Blitz everything until smooth, then set aside.

TO SERVE

Charred Slaw (page 90)

flatbreads (page 91 if you'd like to make your own)

7. Cut the pork into 5cm (2 inch) chunks. Season liberally with salt and pepper.

8. Place the saucepan back over a medium–high heat and drizzle in half the olive oil. Add half the pork and fry for 5 minutes, turning regularly, until browned. Tip onto a plate and repeat with the remaining pork and olive oil. Once all the pork has been browned, tip all the pork from the plate back into the saucepan.

9. Pour in the whizzed sauce, along with the chilli soaking liquid, then add the zest and juice of 1 of the limes and the zest and juice of the orange.

10. Give everything a good stir, then top with a lid and simmer away over a medium heat for 1½ hours. Remove the lid and cook for a further 1½ hours, stirring occasionally, until the pork is completely tender in a rich sauce – it should fall apart when prodded with two forks.

11. Meanwhile, very finely slice your remaining red onion, and put into a small bowl. Season well with salt, then squeeze in the juice of the remaining lime. Use your fingers to scrunch the onion into the lime juice, then set aside to pickle.

12. Once the pork is cooked, pull it into large pieces using two forks. Season to taste, then serve with the pink pickled onions, charred slaw and flatbreads. UNREAL.

*

Tip: The pork and the pickled onions can be made up to the end of step 10, up to 2 days in advance and reheated – the flavour will only improve. This recipe is also a great one for freezing.

Bring it together

→ Make the chipotle pork shoulder (even better made the day before).

→ Start the flatbreads (if making) and quick-pickle the onions.

→ Make the slaw.

→ Finish the flatbreads (if making).

③

① ↑

② →

② Charred Slaw

Charring the cabbage and peppers adds a smoky flavour that complements the spicy slow-cooked pork perfectly. You want to get your pan super hot here, as you are looking to char the veg without cooking it through in order to keep that fresh slaw crunch.

Serves 6   Takes 35 minutes   V/VG/DF/GF

1 white cabbage

1½ tablespoons olive oil

2 mixed peppers (I love a yellow here!)

1 large red onion

2 oranges

large handful of coriander (cilantro)

2–3 tablespoons apple cider vinegar

sea salt

1. Heat a large frying pan over a super-high heat – you want it searingly hot.
2. While the pan is heating, cut the cabbage into quarters lengthways. Season well with salt and drizzle the cut sides with 1 tablespoon of the olive oil, then lay the quarters, with one of the cut sides down, into the pan. Cook until the undersides are blackened, then turn to the second cut sides and char them too – this will take around 6–8 minutes in total.
3. Transfer the cabbage to a chopping board. Put the pan back over the heat.
4. Season the whole peppers and drizzle with the remaining ½ tablespoon olive oil. Add them to the pan and fry for 6 minutes, turning regularly, until the skin is beginning to char in places. Remove from the heat.
5. Finely slice the charred cabbage and put into a bowl, then finely slice the peppers and red onion. Add these to the bowl with the cabbage.
6. Zest both of the oranges into the slaw, then add the juice of one. Cut the skin away from the second orange, then slice into rounds. Add these to the bowl. Roughly chop the coriander (stalks and all) and mix this in, too.
7. Add the apple cider vinegar, then mix the slaw together and season with salt and pepper to taste. Serve alongside the chipotle pork shoulder, with some flatbreads for mopping.

Tip: The slaw can happily be made a couple of hours in advance, and kept covered at room temperature.

③ The Best Flatbreads

My husband, Adam, used to be a baker, and has been making these puffy flatbreads for us for years. They're super easy to make and are perfect for wrapping up all manner of tasty things.

| Makes 12 | Takes 30 minutes, plus proving | V/VG/DF |

¾ teaspoon fast-action dried yeast

½ teaspoon caster (superfine) sugar

400g (14oz) strong white bread flour, plus extra for dusting

1½ tablespoons extra virgin olive oil

1½ teaspoons fine sea salt

1. In a jug, mix together the yeast, sugar and 250ml (9fl oz) warm water. Leave for 5 minutes – this just helps the yeast get nicely hydrated and activated.
2. Tip the remaining ingredients into a large bowl, then pour in the yeasted water. Mix together until it forms a dough, then tip out onto a lightly floured worksurface and knead the dough for 5 minutes until smooth.
3. Put the dough back into the bowl, cover with a clean tea towel and leave for 1½ hours at room temperature until doubled in size.
4. Lightly flour your worksurface again, and divide the dough into 12 even pieces, rolling each one into a tight ball. Place them on a lightly floured baking tray, then cover with the tea towel once more and leave to prove for another 30 minutes until puffy and relaxed.
5. Dust the worksurface with flour once again and use a rolling pin to roll each ball into a 12cm (4½ inch) circle.
6. Heat a frying pan over a medium–high heat, then cook each flatbread for 1 minute on each side until puffed and a little charred. Get a clean tea towel and wrap each cooked flatbread inside it as you go, so they stay warm.

*
Tip: The flatbreads are best eaten straight away, but if you have leftovers, they will keep for 1–2 days, covered tightly. Reheat in the oven for 5 minutes.

Sichuan-Style Aubergines

Move over miso aubergine, there's a new girl in town. Roasted aubergine wedges, glazed in a sticky, spicy, mouth-tingling sauce and topped with crispy shallots, garlic, ginger, nuts and fresh herbs. It's a party in your mouth.

Serves 4–6   Takes 1 hour   V/VG/DF/can be GF

4 aubergines (eggplants)

5 tablespoons neutral oil
(sunflower, vegetable or
light rapeseed)

1 tablespoon cumin seeds

1 tablespoon Sichuan
peppercorns

4 tablespoons soy sauce (use
tamari to make it gluten free)

2 tablespoons black vinegar,
plus a little extra to serve
(if you can't get this, use
balsamic vinegar instead)

2 tablespoons soft
light brown sugar

1–2 tablespoons gochujang

4 fat garlic cloves

large thumb-sized piece
of fresh ginger

3 banana shallots

large handful of mint or
coriander (cilantro) leaves,
or a mixture of both

50g (1¾oz) roasted salted
peanuts or cashews

1–2 red chillies (optional)

cooked rice, to serve

sea salt and freshly ground
black pepper

1. Preheat your oven to 180°C/160°C fan/350°F/gas mark 4.
2. Cut each aubergine into 6 wedges lengthways. Add to a large bowl and lightly season, then drizzle the aubergines with 3 tablespoons of the oil.
3. Place a large frying pan over a medium–high heat. Working in batches, fry the aubergine wedges, cut-sides down, for 2–3 minutes until charred. Transfer to a large roasting tray, cut-side up. Repeat with the remaining wedges.
4. Cover with foil and roast for 35–40 minutes until soft.
5. Meanwhile, toast the cumin seeds and the Sichuan peppercorns in a small saucepan over a medium heat until they smell amazing, then tip into a pestle and mortar. Roughly grind, then return them to the saucepan, along with the soy sauce, vinegar, sugar and gochujang. Finely grate in half the garlic and ginger. Stir, then cook over a medium–high heat for 2–3 minutes until you have a sticky glaze. Take off the heat and set aside.
6. Finely slice the remaining garlic and ginger, along with the shallots, for your crispy topping.
7. Pour the remaining oil into a small frying pan over a high heat. Add the shallots and a pinch of salt. Fry, stirring regularly, for 5–6 minutes until evenly golden. Add the garlic and ginger and fry, stirring, for a minute more until everything is golden and crisp. Remove from the heat.
8. Remove the softened aubergines from the oven and take off the foil, then brush the aubergines all over with the glaze. Increase the oven temperature to 220°C/200°C fan/425°F/gas mark 7 and return the aubergines to the oven for 5 minutes until sticky and caramelised.
9. Tear the herbs. Roughly chop the nuts. Finely slice the red chillies, if using.
10. Pile the sticky aubergines onto a serving platter. Spoon over the crispy topping, then scatter over the herbs and nuts, and the chillies, if using. Serve with rice at the table.

Dad's Roast Ham

Dad makes this ham every Boxing Day, accompanied by a huge tray of dauphinois (if you want to do the same, try my Next-Level Dauphinois on page 82). I'm not sure whether it's the joy of being with all my brothers and the general chaos having a big family brings, but eating it always makes me feel content with life. Of course, it's also f**king delicious, with a crusty caramelised exterior and juicy meat. I love eating it with my fresh celeriac remoulade, opposite.

Makes 1 ham (serves 8, or gives you leftovers for the week)

Takes 2 hours 30 minutes

DF/GF

---

1 onion

handful of cloves

4 bay leaves (fresh or dried are fine)

handful of black peppercorns

2kg (4lb 8oz) smoked boneless gammon joint (get the best quality you can afford – it will make all the difference to the flavour)

250ml (9fl oz) red wine

4 tablespoons English mustard

4 tablespoons demerara sugar

1. Peel the onion and cut it in half, then stud the outsides with the cloves. Put into your largest saucepan, along with the bay leaves and black peppercorns, then place the gammon on top.
2. Pour in the red wine, then top up with enough cold water to just cover the gammon. Bring to the boil over a medium heat, skimming off any white foam that rises to the surface, then simmer gently, uncovered, for 1 hour 20 minutes. Top up with more water if it needs it – you want the gammon to always be just covered in water.
3. Loosely line a roasting tin with foil, leaving enough extra on either side to wrap up around the ham later. Preheat your oven to 200°C/180°C fan/400°F/gas mark 6.
4. Carefully lift the simmered ham into the roasting tin, discarding the cooking liquid. Once cool enough to handle, remove any string, then cut off the outer layer of skin and discard. Using a small, sharp knife, score a criss-cross pattern into the fat, taking care not to cut into the meat itself.
5. Spoon the mustard all over the ham, then scatter over the sugar so that the ham gets covered in a mustardy sugar crust. Wrap up in the foil parcel and roast for 20 minutes, then uncover and roast for a further 15–20 minutes until the ham is sticky and caramelised.
6. Leave to cool before slicing. Honestly, once you've made your own ham, you'll never look back.

*
Tip: The ham will keep happily in the fridge for a week, well wrapped.

Celeriac Remoulade

This classic creamy, mustardy salad with nutty celeriac is a winter winner. I've added pink grapefruit for a zingy freshness, and cornichons to cut through the richness of the ham. The initial chopping is a bit of a ball-ache, but once made, it keeps great in the fridge, perfect for a quick munch.

Serves 8 (or gives you leftovers)

Takes 40 minutes

V/DF/GF

1 medium celeriac

150g (5½oz) mayonnaise

2 tablespoons Dijon mustard

1 tablespoon apple cider vinegar or white wine vinegar

handful of mixed herbs (I love dill and chives or parsley here)

3 large handfuls of cornichons

2 pink grapefruits

freshly ground black pepper

1. Peel and finely slice the celeriac, then cut each slice into fine matchsticks and tip into your largest bowl. Add the mayonnaise, mustard and vinegar, and mix well so that each piece of celeriac gets coated in the dressing – I find using my hands here is the most effective way.
2. Roughly chop the herbs (stalks and all) and finely slice the cornichons. Add both to the remoulade, and toss together.
3. Cut the ends off the grapefruits, then use a sharp knife to cut away the peel and slice each grapefruit into segments – if you segment the grapefruit over the celeriac remoulade, you can save all those tasty juices. Add the segments to the remoulade and gently fold together.
4. Season to taste – I like lots of freshly cracked black pepper – then serve with Dad's Roast Ham, opposite.

*
Tip: The remoulade can be made a couple of days before; it will happily keep in the fridge.

Sicilian-Vibes Fish Stew

I first ate a version of this over at my friend Claud's house and became obsessed with the combination of fresh fish with salty capers and pops of sweet dried fruit that had plumped in the rich tomato sauce. To add another dimension, I've confited (slow-cooked in oil) some garlic at the start, which is then used in both the stew and aioli – if you can't be bothered, you can always leave that bit out, replacing it with garlic to taste instead.

Serves 4–6   Takes 1 hour 30 minutes   DF

1 large banana shallot
or 1 onion

1 fennel bulb

3 celery stalks

2 tablespoons olive oil
(or garlic confit oil if made
in advance)

handful of parsley

2 teaspoons smoked paprika

1 tablespoon fennel seeds

250ml (9fl oz) white wine

2 × 400g (14oz) tins
plum tomatoes

big pinch of saffron
(optional but delicious)

75g (2¾oz) sultanas or raisins

4 tablespoons capers

1 lemon

pinch of caster (superfine)
sugar (optional)

400g (14oz) skinless and
boneless white fish (I like a
firmer fish here, such as hake)

1. To make the confit garlic, peel the garlic cloves and put them into a small saucepan. Pour in enough olive oil to just cover the garlic. Add the chilli flakes, then peel in the lemon rind. Place the pan over a low heat and gently cook away until the garlic is completely soft – this will take around 25–30 minutes. Once soft, set aside. (This confit garlic can be prepared a week or so in advance and kept in a jar with the oil.)

2. Meanwhile, finely chop the shallot or onion, fennel and celery. Scrape all the veg into your largest saucepan, along with a big pinch of salt. Add the olive oil (if you have made the confit garlic in advance, use some of the oil from this!). Cook over a medium heat, stirring occasionally, for 8–10 minutes until the veg are soft.

3. Chop the parsley stalks and add to the pan, along with 4 of the confit garlic cloves, the smoked paprika and fennel seeds. Cook, smooshing the garlic, for a minute more.

4. Pour in the white wine. Once bubbled away by half, add the tomatoes, along with 1½ tins of water, and the saffron, if using.

5. Leave the stew base to bubble away, still over a medium heat, for 30 minutes, stirring occasionally. Then add the dried fruit and cook for 15 minutes more until the tomatoes are broken down and the sauce is rich and delicious.

6. Stir the capers through the sauce and add the juice of 1 lemon, then season to taste with salt, pepper and a pinch of sugar if it needs it. Remember the fish will add a salty brininess later.

800g (1lb 12oz) seafood of your choice (this could be prawns, clams, mussels or a mixture)

6 tablespoons mayonnaise

crusty bread (I love a fat baguette), to serve

sea salt and freshly ground black pepper

FOR THE CONFIT GARLIC

1 garlic bulb

around 250ml (9fl oz) olive oil (don't worry, you won't be eating all of it!)

big pinch of chilli flakes, plus extra to serve (optional)

1 lemon

7. Cut the fish into large chunks and season. Clean your seafood, pulling the 'beards' out of the mussels, if using. Put everything into the stew base, cover with a lid and cook for 5–8 minutes until everything is cooked through.

8. Meanwhile, spoon the mayo into a small bowl. Grate in the zest from the remaining lemon, then smoosh in as many confit garlic cloves as you like to make your cheat's aioli. Season with salt, pepper and lemon juice to taste.

9. Roughly chop the parsley leaves, scatter over the stew, then drizzle over some confit garlic oil and a few chilli flakes, if you like. Serve with the cheat's aioli and some crusty bread for dipping. Properly delicious.

Tip: You can prepare the base (up to the end of step 5) up to a day in advance, then reheat when ready to eat.

Confit Garlic

↑

page 96

**Sicilian-Vibes
Fish Stew**

↑

page 96

Soy-Glazed Pork Belly with Wedding Salad & Coconut Rice

① Soy Pork Belly

I first made this as a date-night dinner and was hyped to find that the crackling came out unbelievably well. Better yet, the pork cooks in its own delicious sauce: a thin soy 'gravy' that gets soaked up by the coconut rice.

Serves 4   Takes 3 hours   DF/can be GF

1kg (2lb 4oz) boneless pork belly joint

2 teaspoons vegetable or rapeseed oil

½ ripe pineapple (use the other half in the Malaysian Wedding Salad, opposite)

1 red onion

thumb-sized piece of fresh ginger

6 garlic cloves

3 star anise

400ml (14fl oz) chicken stock

3 tablespoons soy sauce (use tamari to make it gluten free)

2 tablespoons soft brown sugar

2 tablespoons rice wine vinegar

sea salt and freshly ground black pepper

1. The night before you want to cook, score the pork belly by making diagonal cuts through the skin. Try to avoid cutting into the meat itself.

2. Place the pork on a wire rack over a deep roasting tray. Boil half a kettle, then pour the water all over the skin. Drain the water, then pat the pork dry with paper towels and transfer to a large plate or tray. Leave uncovered in the fridge to dry out overnight. This is the secret to crispy crackling!

3. The next day, preheat your oven to 220°C/200°C fan/ 425°F/gas mark 7. Remove the pork from the fridge to come up to room temperature. Lightly rub the skin with the oil and season well on all sides with salt and pepper.

4. Slice the pineapple, into rounds, then cut the red onion into wedges and roughly chop the ginger. Arrange in the bottom of a high-sided roasting tin, along with the garlic and star anise.

5. Place the pork joint on top and roast for 45 minutes.

6. Meanwhile, stir together the stock, soy sauce, sugar and vinegar in a jug.

7. After 45 minutes, reduce the oven temperature to 160°C/140°C fan/325°F/gas mark 3 and pour the sauce into the roasting tin around the pork, being careful not to get any liquid on the crackling. The meat should now be mostly submerged in the liquid, with the crackling above it.

8. Roast for another 1½ hours, then increase the oven temperature to 220°C/200°C fan/425°F/gas mark 7 and cook for a further 15–20 minutes until the meat is super tender in its own sauce and the crackling looks unreal.

9. Transfer the pork to a board to rest for 20 minutes (this is the perfect time to make your coconut rice) and reserve the cooked pineapple. Meanwhile, strain the sauce into a saucepan and skim off any noticeable bits of fat.

10. When you're ready to eat, cut the pork belly into 4 pieces and reheat the sauce. Serve the pork belly with the Coconut Rice and Malaysian Wedding Salad, along with the reserved pineapple and sauce on the side for pouring. Tasty AF.

② Malaysian Wedding Salad

I first tried a version of this at the Malaysian restaurant Normah's in London. The combination of cucumber, pineapple, vinegary onions and chilli cuts through the pork belly perfectly.

Serves 4   Takes 15 minutes   V/VG/DF/GF

1 cucumber

½ ripe pineapple

1 red onion

1 bird's eye chilli

2–3 tablespoons rice vinegar

½ teaspoon caster (superfine) sugar

large handful of coriander (cilantro)

1. Halve the cucumber lengthways and remove its seedy core with a teaspoon (I usually then eat this rather than chucking it away – weird?), then cut into thin diagonals. Slice the pineapple into thin bite-sized wedges, then very finely slice the red onion and chilli. Scrape everything into a salad bowl.

2. Add the rice vinegar and caster sugar and toss everything to combine, then season to taste. (The salad can sit like this for up to 2 hours.)

3. When you're ready to serve, roughly tear the coriander (stalks and all). Mix through the salad.

4. Eat with the Soy Pork Belly and Coconut Rice for the ultimate Sunday meal.

③ Coconut Rice

There's something so comforting about coconut rice. Be sure to wash the grains of rice properly; I know it feels like a faff, but it's the secret to fluffiness.

Serves 4   Takes 30 minutes   V/VG/DF/GF

300g (10½oz) jasmine rice

400ml (14fl oz) tin full-fat coconut milk

sea salt

1. Tip the rice into a large bowl. Fill with cold water and use your fingers to agitate the grains of rice. The water will turn cloudy. Drain through a sieve and repeat a couple more times until the water stays clear, then drain the rice and tip into a medium saucepan with a well-fitting lid.
2. Add the tin of coconut milk and 150ml (5fl oz) cold water, along with a big pinch of salt.
3. Place the pan over a medium heat and bring to the boil. Once boiling, put on the lid and cook for 10 minutes, then turn off the heat, and leave the rice, with the lid still on, to steam for a further 10 minutes until cooked through and fluffy.
4. Serve with the Soy Pork Belly and Malaysian Wedding Salad.

Bring it together

→ Prep your pork belly the night before for the crispiest crackling.

→ Start cooking the Soy Pork Belly.

→ Make the Malaysian Wedding Salad up to step 2 (it can then sit for up to 2 hours).

→ Cook the Coconut Rice and add the coriander to the salad.

Sunday

④

~Reset~

Chicken & Avocado Grain Bowl

If there's one recipe that's going to make you feel bloody excellent, it's this: grains tossed in herby guac dressing, served with the juiciest cumin-crusted chicken, which is bathed in a chilli and lime marinade.

Serves 2   Takes 30 minutes   DF

1 ripe avocado

large handful of basil

3 spring onions (scallions)

1 green chilli

1 garlic clove

2 teaspoons ground cumin

2 limes

125g (4½oz) dried grains or 250g (9oz) pouch ready-cooked grains (brown rice would also work well if that's easier)

2 good-quality skinless, boneless chicken breasts

3½ tablespoons extra virgin olive oil, plus a little extra for drizzling

200g (7oz) green vegetables of your choice (I like fine green beans, sugar snaps, mange tout/snow peas or asparagus tips)

2 large handfuls of baby spinach leaves

sea salt and freshly ground black pepper

1. Scoop half the avocado flesh into a blender or small food processor, along with most of the basil. Roughly chop 2 of the spring onions (both green and white parts) and add these as well. Add half the chilli to the blender, along with the garlic, 1 teaspoon of the cumin, the zest and juice of 1 lime and 7 tablespoons water. Blitz to form a thick, smooth dressing, season to taste and set aside.

2. If using dried grains, cook according to the packet instructions.

3. Place the chicken breasts between two sheets of baking paper and bash with a rolling pin until 2cm (¾ inch) thick.

4. Heat a griddle or non-stick frying pan over a high heat.

5. While the pan heats, season the bashed chicken all over with salt, pepper and the remaining 1 teaspoon cumin. Drizzle with a little olive oil, then lay the chicken breasts into the hot pan. Cook for 3–4 minutes on each side until cooked through, juicy and charred.

6. Meanwhile, in a wide, shallow bowl, combine the zest and juice of the remaining lime with 3 tablespoons of the olive oil. Finely chop the remaining chilli and add this too. Season.

7. Transfer the cooked chicken to the bowl with the chilli-lime marinade. Leave to cool and reverse-marinate for flavour.

8. Return the pan to a high heat. Toss your chosen green veg in the remaining ½ tablespoon olive oil, then season and add to the hot pan. Cook for 3–4 minutes until just tender and charred. Remove from the heat.

9. Finely slice the remaining spring onion. Cube the remaining avo half and, if using ready-cooked grains, heat them now.

10. Tip the cooked grains into a large bowl, then add the avo dressing, spinach leaves and charred greens. Stir to combine.

11. Divide the dressed grains between two bowls. Slice the cooked chicken and place on top, along with the cubed avo. Spoon over the chicken marinade, then scatter over the spring onions and remaining basil, to serve.

Sabich Salad

A *sabich* is an Israeli sandwich, made with pitta and stuffed with sticky fried aubergine, boiled egg, pickles, chopped salad and hummus. I've taken many of the components and turned it into a super-moreish salad. This one's dedicated to my best friend Yas, whose love for Middle Eastern food knows no bounds...

Serves 2 | Takes 30 minutes | V/DF

1 large aubergine (eggplant)

2 medium eggs

1½ tablespoons olive oil

2 tablespoons mango chutney, plus extra to serve

4 dollops of hummus (you can use homemade or a good-quality shop-bought one here)

pickles of your choice, to serve (I love Turkish green peppers and/or pickled red cabbage with this)

sea salt and freshly ground black pepper

FOR THE CHOPPED SALAD

½ red onion

1 Baby Gem lettuce

2 vine tomatoes or 2 handfuls of cherry tomatoes

½ cucumber

handful of radishes (optional but delicious)

handful of mixed herbs (parsley, dill, mint, coriander/cilantro and basil would all work well)

juice of 1 lemon

2–3 teaspoons sumac (to taste)

2 tablespoons olive oil

1. Cut the aubergine into rounds 2cm (¾ inch) thick. Season well with salt and set aside in a sieve over a bowl while you make the chopped salad.

2. For the salad, finely chop the red onion and scrape into a bowl. Chop the Baby Gem, tomatoes and cucumber, and add these too. Finely slice the radishes, if using, and finely chop your mixed herbs. Add these to the bowl. Squeeze in the lemon juice, then add the sumac and olive oil. Toss together, season to taste.

3. Bring a small saucepan of water to the boil and set a large frying pan over a high heat. Once the water is boiling, add the whole eggs and set a timer for 6 minutes – you want them to be jammy.

4. Lay the aubergine slices into the hot pan. Drizzle over the oil, then fry for 3 minutes on each side until deeply golden and soft. Brush the aubergine slices with the mango chutney and cook for a further 1–2 minutes until sticky and caramelised. Remove from the heat.

5. Drain and cool the eggs, then peel and halve.

6. Spread the hummus across the bases of two plates. Pile on the chopped salad, glazed aubergine, soft-boiled eggs and pickles. Serve with another spoonful of mango chutney, if you like. Unreal.

Hummus, Pomegranate Slaw & Pitta Chips

This is our go-to meal for an injection of *all* the veg. I can't even tell you how many times I've made this pomegranate slaw – it's an absolute staple in my house, and so good. Homemade hummus is one of the easiest, most satisfying things to make. You'll wonder why you ever bought it ready-made.

Serves 2 | Takes 30 minutes | V/VG/DF

2 pitta breads (I often use pitta bread straight from the freezer for this!)

1 tablespoon olive oil, plus extra for drizzling

1 tablespoon za'atar

sea salt and freshly ground black pepper

FOR THE HUMMUS

400g (14oz) tin chickpeas

3 tablespoons tahini

½ teaspoon ground cumin

juice of ½ lemon

FOR THE POMEGRANATE SLAW

¼ red cabbage

1 carrot

1 pepper (any colour will do)

½ cucumber

2 spring onions (scallions) – optional but delicious

handful of mixed herbs (I like parsley, mint, coriander/ cilantro or dill)

juice of ½ lemon

2 tablespoons pomegranate molasses

½ teaspoon ground cumin

2 teaspoons za'atar

1. Preheat your oven to 200°C/180°C fan/400°F/gas mark 6.
2. To make the hummus, drain the chickpea liquid into a small bowl and reserve. Tip the chickpeas into a blender or small food processor, then add the tahini, cumin and lemon juice. Pour in half of the reserved chickpea liquid and blitz until you have a smooth, super-creamy hummus. If the hummus is still a little too thick, add another splash of the chickpea liquid and blitz again – depending on the variety of chickpeas, you may use all the liquid. Once you're happy with the consistency, season to taste, spoon into a bowl, drizzle with some olive oil, and set aside.
3. Using scissors, cut the pitta breads into random shards. Tip the pitta chips onto a roasting tray, toss them with the olive oil, za'atar and a pinch of salt, then spread out into a single layer so they roast evenly. Bake for 8–10 minutes, flipping halfway, until golden and super crisp.
4. Meanwhile, make the pomegranate slaw. Very finely slice the cabbage (or you can use the coarse side of a grater if that's easier). Scrape into a large bowl.
5. Cut the carrot into matchsticks (or, again, use the grater if easier). Finely slice the pepper, cucumber and spring onions, if using. Roughly chop the herbs (stalks and all, unless using mint). Add all these to the bowl with the cabbage.
6. Add the lemon juice, pomegranate molasses, cumin and za'atar. Toss the slaw together with your hands, season to taste and add a drizzle of olive oil, if you like.
7. Serve the slaw with the hummus and pitta chips for dipping, topped with a little extra olive oil and za'atar if you like.

Sabich Salad

↓

page 110

**Hummus,
Pomegranate Slaw
& Pitta Chips**

↑

page 111

Pea, Feta & Hazelnut Risotto

This is one of my bestie Pops's favourite meals. It's one that I cook when we're all in need of a pick-me-up; there's something about eating a vivid green bowl of food that can't fail to make you smile. The secret here is blitzing half the peas into a purée, and stirring it through the risotto at the end. It's super fresh and vibrant.

Serves 2

Takes 45 minutes

can be V (if using alternative cheese) / GF

large handful of hazelnuts (blanched hazelnuts are ideal, but no stress if you can't get them)

300g (10½oz) frozen peas

1 banana shallot or 1 small onion

1 tablespoon olive oil

2 garlic cloves

handful of mint

150g (5½oz) risotto rice (arborio or carnaroli work well)

150ml (5fl oz) white wine

600–700ml (21–24fl oz) boiling vegetable stock

1–2 tablespoons sherry vinegar or white wine vinegar

30g (1oz) parmesan or veggie alternative

100g (3½oz) feta

Tabasco, to serve (optional)

squeeze of lemon juice, to serve (optional)

sea salt and freshly ground black pepper

1. Toast the hazelnuts in a small dry frying pan over a medium heat until lightly golden, then set aside.
2. Weigh out your frozen peas into a bowl and set aside to defrost.
3. Finely chop the shallot or onion.
4. Heat the olive oil in a frying pan over a medium heat. Add the shallot or onion, along with a pinch of salt. Cook, stirring regularly, for 8–10 minutes until softened but not coloured.
5. Meanwhile, finely chop the garlic cloves, roughly chop the toasted hazelnuts, and pick the mint leaves.
6. Add the garlic to the frying pan and cook for 1 minute more, then tip in the rice. Stir everything together, toast for a minute or so, then pour in the white wine.
7. Once the wine has been absorbed by the rice, add a ladleful of vegetable stock. Cook, stirring regularly, until the stock has been absorbed, then repeat. Keep adding the stock until most of it has been absorbed and the rice is tender with a slight bite; this will take around 20–25 minutes.
8. Meanwhile, tip half the peas into a blender, along with 1 tablespoon of the vinegar, most of the mint, plenty of salt and pepper and 100ml (3½fl oz) water. Blitz to form a smooth, vivid green purée. (If you prefer, you can do this in a bowl using a handheld stick blender.)
9. Once the rice is tender, stir through the pea purée and the remaining whole peas. Finely grate in the parmesan and stir until everything is heated through. Season to taste, adding a little more vinegar if you like.
10. Dish up the risotto between two bowls, then crumble over the feta and scatter over the toasted hazelnuts and the remaining mint leaves. I like to finish it with a splash of Tabasco and a squeeze of lemon, to serve.

Sticky Soy Veg & Fried Egg Rice

A fried egg on cooked white rice with some chilli oil stands alone as a thing of beauty, but if you add to that some shredded stir-fried cabbage, carrots and spring onions, along with soy, Shaoxing and sesame oil, you have a meal you'll be making on repeat.

Serves 2   Takes 30 minutes   V/DF/can be GF

150g (5½oz) basmati rice

½ small cabbage (hispi/
pointed, savoy or Chinese
all work perfectly)

4 spring onions (scallions)

4 carrots

2 tablespoons sesame oil

2 tablespoons kecap manis
(or use regular soy sauce or
tamari + 1 teaspoon honey –
use tamari to make it
gluten free)

1 tablespoon Shaoxing
wine or dry sherry

2 medium eggs

handful of salted nuts
(cashews or peanuts)

crispy chilli oil, to serve
(make your own on page 192
or use Lee Kum Kee)

1. Cook your rice according to the packet instructions.
2. Meanwhile, finely slice the cabbage and spring onions (both green and white parts), and cut the carrots into matchsticks. (If you can't be bothered to matchstick, just peel the carrots into ribbons instead – it is Sunday, after all!)
3. Heat a large frying pan over a high heat. Pour in 1 tablespoon of the sesame oil, then add the cabbage, spring onions and carrots. Fry for 4–5 minutes until softened, then add the kecap manis (or soy sauce/tamari and honey), along with the Shaoxing wine (or sherry) and 1 tablespoon water. Stir so that the veg gets coated in the sticky sauce, then scrape everything over to one half of the frying pan.
4. Pour the remaining 1 tablespoon sesame oil into the empty half of the pan, then crack in the eggs. Fry to your liking. Meanwhile, chop the nuts.
5. Once the rice is cooked, divide between two bowls. Top each with a pile of the sticky veg and a fried egg, then scatter over the nuts. Spoon over the crispy chilli oil to serve. Easy win.

Spiced Aubergine Rice Salad

Rice salads often feature on my private cheffing menus. The rice absorbs all the spices and flavour, making each mouthful bang. In this one, there's fried aubergine, herbs and the freshest ginger, lime and coconut dressing. It will sort you out.

Serves 2 | Takes 35 minutes | V/VG/GF

125g (4½oz) basmati and wild rice, or a 250g (9oz) pre-cooked basmati and wild rice pouch

handful of mint

thumb-sized piece of fresh ginger

5 tablespoons coconut yogurt

½–1 green chilli (depending on how spicy you like it)

zest and juice of 1 lime

large handful of coriander (cilantro)

1 red onion

1 large aubergine (eggplant)

1½ tablespoons rapeseed or other neutral oil

2 fat garlic cloves

2 teaspoons each of mustard seeds and cumin seeds (change this up and use whatever whole spices you fancy)

½ cucumber

large handful of salted nuts (I love cashews here)

sea salt and freshly ground black pepper

1. If using dried rice, cook according to the packet instructions, then drain.
2. Meanwhile, pick half the mint leaves and chop half of your ginger into small pieces. Put both into a blender or small food processor, along with the coconut yogurt, green chilli, lime zest and half the coriander (stalks and all). Blitz to create a vivid green dressing, then season with salt, pepper and lime juice to taste. Set aside.
3. Finely slice the red onion and cut the aubergine into cubes.
4. Heat the oil in a large frying pan over a medium heat. Add the onion and aubergine and cook for 8–10 minutes, stirring occasionally, until the aubergine is soft and caramelised.
5. Finely grate the garlic and remaining ginger into the pan. Cook, stirring, for 1 minute more, then spoon in the whole spices. Continue to cook, still stirring, for a further minute until it smells amazing, then tip everything into a large bowl.
6. Dice the cucumber. Pick the remaining mint leaves and roughly chop the remaining coriander (stalks and all). Roughly chop the nuts. Add the cucumber, mint, nuts and coriander to the aubergine mixture.
7. If using a pouch of pre-cooked rice, heat it now.
8. Tip the cooked rice into the bowl with everything else. Stir well to combine, then season with salt, pepper and lime juice to taste.
9. Divide the yogurt dressing between the bases of two bowls, then pile on the spiced aubergine rice to serve.

Roasted Carrot Soup with Sesame Halloumi Croutons

Soup is a staple in our flat. It never fails to blow my mind the flavour you get out of roasted veg. Here, I've gone for classic carrot with some cumin, garlic and pomegranate molasses for a tangy kick. Plus there are spicy sesame cheese 'croutons' on top, because why not?

Serves 2	Takes 45 minutes	V/can be VG/GF

500g (1lb 2oz) carrots

1 onion

3 fat garlic cloves

2 tablespoons olive oil

1 tablespoon cumin seeds

800ml (28fl oz) vegetable stock

2 tablespoons pomegranate molasses, plus extra to serve

225g (8oz) halloumi (see Tip)

1 tablespoon sesame seeds

big pinch of chilli flakes (optional)

handful of coriander (cilantro), dill or parsley

sea salt and freshly ground black pepper

1. Preheat your oven to 220°C/200°C fan/425°F/gas mark 7.
2. Peel your carrots (no need to do this if they're really fresh), then chop into medium-sized chunks. Cut the onion into 8 wedges. Peel the garlic cloves, keeping them whole.
3. In a large roasting tray, toss the carrots, onion and garlic cloves with the olive oil, cumin seeds and plenty of seasoning, then spread into a single layer so that everything roasts evenly. Roast for 20–25 minutes until soft and caramelised.
4. Once the veg is roasted, heat up the vegetable stock in a medium-sized saucepan. Add the roasted veg, then blitz with a handheld blender until smooth. If you like a thinner soup, add a splash of water. Season with 1 tablespoon pomegranate molasses, and salt and pepper to taste.
5. Cut the halloumi into crouton-sized cubes (up to you how big or small you make these).
6. Heat a large frying pan over a medium–high heat and add the halloumi. Fry for 3–4 minutes, turning regularly until the cubes are evenly golden and crisp on all sides, then drizzle with the remaining 1 tablespoon pomegranate molasses while still in the pan. Once the croutons are evenly glazed, scatter over the sesame seeds and chilli flakes, if using, so that each piece of cheese gets covered. Take off heat.
7. Reheat the soup and roughly chop the herbs (stalks and all). Divide the soup between two wide, shallow bowls. Top with the halloumi croutons, along with the herbs and a drizzle of pomegranate molasses. Serve.

*

Tip: For a vegan alternative, use tofu instead of halloumi.

Turmeric & Apricot Giant Couscous

There was a spiced giant couscous and apricot salad on the menu at the first place I worked as a chef: Marmadukes café in Sheffield. I love the combo just as much now. To make this a bit special, you quick-pickle a shallot in turmeric and lemon, then use it to make an unreal zingy dressing for the couscous.

Serves 2 | Takes 35 minutes | V/VG (if using maple syrup and no feta)

500g (1lb 2oz) carrots

4 tablespoons extra virgin olive oil

1 tablespoon cumin seeds

2 teaspoons smoked paprika (use hot smoked if you like heat)

1 banana shallot

1 small garlic clove

½ teaspoon ground turmeric

zest and juice of 1 lemon

3 teaspoons honey or maple syrup

150g (5½oz) giant couscous

75g (1¾oz) dried apricots

large handful of mixed herbs (use any combo you like here – dill, coriander/cilantro, mint and parsley are all banging)

100g (3½oz) feta (optional)

sea salt and freshly ground black pepper

1. Preheat your oven to 220°C/200°C fan/425°F/gas mark 7.
2. Peel the carrots (no need to do this if they're really fresh). Cut into medium-sized chunks and tip onto a large roasting tray. Toss with 1 tablespoon of the olive oil, along with the cumin seeds, paprika and plenty of seasoning, then spread out into a single layer so they roast evenly. Roast for 20 minutes.
3. Meanwhile, very finely slice the shallot, then scrape into a large salad bowl. Finely grate in the garlic, then add the turmeric, lemon zest and juice, and 2 teaspoons of the honey or maple syrup. Stir and season well with salt and plenty of black pepper. Set aside for the shallot to soften.
4. Next, cook the giant couscous according to the packet instructions and drain. Roughly chop the dried apricots and herbs (stalks and all unless using mint).
5. Once the carrots have been cooking for 20 minutes, drizzle over the remaining 1 teaspoon of honey or maple syrup and toss to coat. Return to the oven for a further 3–5 minutes until nicely caramelised.
6. Stir the remaining 3 tablespoons extra virgin olive oil into the bowl with the turmeric shallot mixture to create your dressing. Add the couscous and cooked carrots, along with all their spiced goodness from the tray, then add the apricots and most of the herbs. Toss together and season to taste.
7. Divide between two bowls. Crumble over the feta, if using, and scatter over the remaining herbs to serve.

Honeyed Halloumi Salad

Honey and halloumi were meant to be together; it's that salty-sweet combo that we all know and love. For this salad, I've made a chilli and caper dressing that perfectly brings together the crunchy raw veg and charred courgette. It's a proper banger.

Serves 2   Takes 25 minutes   V/GF

3 tablespoons pumpkin seeds (pepitas)

1 large courgette (zucchini)

1 tablespoon olive oil

100g (3½oz) mange tout (snow peas)

200g (7oz) radishes

225g (8oz) halloumi

1 tablespoon honey

2 large handfuls of rocket (arugula)

sea salt and freshly ground black pepper

FOR THE DRESSING

½–1 red or green chilli

2 tablespoons capers

zest and juice of 1 lemon

3 tablespoons extra virgin olive oil

1–2 teaspoons honey

1. Toast the pumpkin seeds in a large dry frying pan until beginning to pop. Season, then tip into a small bowl and set aside.
2. To make the dressing, finely chop the chilli and scrape into a second small bowl. Chop the capers and add these to the bowl as well. Add the lemon zest and half the lemon juice, along with the olive oil and 1 teaspoon of the honey. Whisk together to form your dressing. Season to taste, adding more honey and lemon juice if needed. Set aside.
3. Cut the courgette into thick half-moons and put into a large bowl. Drizzle over the olive oil and season with salt and pepper, then toss to combine.
4. Heat the same frying pan used to toast the seeds over a high heat. Fry the courgette in two batches for around 2 minutes on each side until tender and nicely charred. Divide the charred courgette between two plates, and, while still hot, squeeze over some of the remaining lemon juice.
5. Finely slice the raw mange tout lengthways (keeping it raw gives the freshest crunch) and roughly chop the radishes. Set aside.
6. Return the same frying pan to a medium–high heat. Slice the halloumi and add it to the pan. Fry for 1–2 minutes on each side until golden and crisp, then drizzle over the honey. Cook for a further minute or so until each piece of cheese is sticky and caramelised, then take off the heat.
7. Scatter the rocket over the charred courgette, then top with the mange tout and radishes. Spoon the dressing over each salad, then place the honeyed halloumi on top and sprinkle over the pumpkin seeds, to serve.

Cheddar & Chilli Jam Crouton Salad

This salad is inspired by a good ol' classic cheese salad sandwich – with pickles, of course. I made chilli jam croutons on a whim one lunchtime; I wanted a bit of spice, saw an open jar of chilli jam in the fridge and thought, Why not? The result? Sticky, spicy, caramelised bread. Game-changer.

Serves 2   Takes 20 minutes   V

3 thick slices of white bread (I like sourdough, ciabatta or crusty white)

5 tablespoons extra virgin olive oil

2 tablespoons chilli jam

1 teaspoon Dijon or wholegrain mustard

1–2 tablespoons sherry or balsamic vinegar

around 100g (3½oz) whatever salad leaves you like (chicory/witlof, Cos or Baby Gem all work great here)

½ cucumber

150g (5½oz) cherry tomatoes

100g (3½oz) extra-mature cheddar

2 large handfuls cornichons or gherkins

sea salt and freshly ground black pepper

1. Cut the bread into rough croutons. Toss in a salad bowl with 2 tablespoons of the olive oil and season with salt and pepper.

2. Heat a frying pan over a medium–high heat. Add the croutons to the pan and fry, turning regularly, for 4–5 minutes until crisp. Take off the heat, then add the chilli jam, stirring so that each crouton gets nicely coated and a little sticky. Leave to cool in the pan.

3. Add the mustard and vinegar to the bowl you used to toss the croutons (no need to wash up in between!), then pour in the remaining 3 tablespoons olive oil. Whisk together to create your dressing, and season to taste.

4. Slice your salad leaves, chop the cucumber and halve the cherry tomatoes. Add to the dressing. Very finely slice the cheddar into thin shavings. Finely slice the cornichons or gherkins, then add these to the bowl, along with the cheddar shavings and cooled chilli jam croutons.

5. Toss the salad together, then divide between two bowls to serve. Fried bread + cheese + pickles = excellent salad.

Charred Broccoli & Kimchi Rice Bowl

This dish, strangely enough, was inspired by a side my best mate Haz and I had with some takeaway sushi. Charred broccoli was coated in this INCREDIBLE dressing, which was creamy with tahini, and seasoned with soy, fried garlic, ginger, chilli and a hint of sweetness. Here, I've paired it with rice and a side of kimchi for some tang. Anna, my friend and recipe-tester, has made it multiple times!

Serves 2　　　　　　Takes 30 minutes　　　　　　DF/can be GF

150g (5½oz) brown rice

1 head of broccoli

2 fat garlic cloves

½–1 red or green chilli (depending on how spicy you like it)

2 tablespoons vegetable or rapeseed oil

thumb-sized piece of fresh ginger

3 tablespoons tahini

1 tablespoon dark soy sauce (use tamari to make it gluten free)

1–2 teaspoons maple syrup or agave nectar

1–2 teaspoons rice wine vinegar

200g (7oz) sugar snap peas or mange tout (snow peas)

kimchi, to serve

1 tablespoon sesame seeds

sea salt

1. Cook the rice according to the packet instructions.
2. Meanwhile, bring a medium-sized saucepan of salted water to the boil. Cut the broccoli head into large florets and roughly chop the stalk.
3. Drop the broccoli into the boiling salted water and cook for 2 minutes, then drain into a sieve and leave to steam dry.
4. Finely chop the garlic and chilli. Heat 1 tablespoon of the oil in a large non-stick frying pan over a medium–high heat. Add the garlic and chilli and fry, stirring, for 1 minute or so until the garlic is lightly golden. Scrape the contents of the pan into a small bowl.
5. Finely grate the ginger into the bowl, then add the tahini, soy sauce and 2 tablespoons water. Stir together to create your dressing. Season with the maple syrup or agave and the rice wine vinegar to taste, adding a splash more water if needed; you want it to be drizzle-able. Set aside.
6. Return the frying pan to a high heat (no need to wash it in between). Drizzle in the remaining 1 tablespoon oil. Add the broccoli and sugar snap peas or mange tout. Fry for 4–6 minutes, turning regularly, until nicely charred. Remove from the heat.
7. Divide the cooked rice between two bowls. Spoon on a pile of kimchi, then top with the charred greens. Drizzle over the dressing and scatter over the sesame seeds to serve.

Blackened Cajun Salmon Pittas

My wonderful friend Maz came back from a work trip raving about these blackened salmon sandwiches she'd had. This got my brain whirring, so I decided to coat salmon in Cajun seasoning, char it and shove it into a pitta with a courgette and coriander slaw (feat. hot-sauce sunflower seeds) and a limey yogurt.

Serves 2

Takes 25 minutes

2 teaspoons olive oil

2 skinless, boneless salmon fillets

3 teaspoons Cajun seasoning

2 large or 4 small pittas

lime wedges, to serve

sea salt and freshly ground black pepper

FOR THE SLAW

3 tablespoons sunflower seeds

1–2 teaspoons hot sauce, depending on how spicy you like it (I love Cholula here), plus extra to serve

1 large courgette (zucchini)

4 spring onions (scallions)

large handful of coriander (cilantro)

juice of 1 lime

1 tablespoon extra virgin olive oil

FOR THE LIMEY YOGURT

1 tablespoon hot sauce

150g (5½oz) Greek or natural yogurt

zest and juice of 1 lime

1. To make the slaw, toast the sunflower seeds in a small, dry frying pan over a medium heat until lightly golden and beginning to pop. Take the pan off the heat and add the hot sauce. Toss together and tip into a large bowl.

2. Peel the courgette into long ribbons and add to the bowl with the sunflower seeds. Finely chop the courgette core, and add that too. Finely slice the spring onions (both green and white parts), and roughly chop the coriander (stalks and all). Add these to the bowl, along with the lime juice and olive oil. Toss together and season to taste, then set aside.

3. To make the limey yogurt, stir together the hot sauce and yogurt in a bowl. Add the lime zest, then season with salt, pepper and lime juice to taste. Set aside.

4. For the salmon, drizzle the olive oil generously over the salmon fillets. Season, then evenly coat each fillet in 1 teaspoon of the Cajun seasoning.

5. Heat a non-stick frying pan over a high heat. Once visibly hot, add the salmon to the pan, then reduce the heat to medium. Fry for 6–8 minutes, turning every 2 minutes so that the salmon evenly blackens and cooks through; you want it to flake into large chunks. Take the pan off the heat and sprinkle over the remaining 1 teaspoon Cajun seasoning.

6. Toast the pittas and cut each one in half. Spoon the yogurt into the pitta halves, then pile in the courgette slaw and flake in the blackened salmon. Serve with lime wedges for squeezing and, if you like things spicy, a little more hot sauce. Unreal.

Peanut Butter Dal with Tomato Broccoli Tarka

Dal is the thing I make when I'm in need of some nourishment – the colour alone always makes me feel happy. I once added a spoonful of peanut butter into the mix – bastardised it may be, but it bangs. I always like to add some veg, too, so I've chucked some broc and cherry toms into the tarka.

Serves 2   Takes 45 minutes   V/VG/DF/can be GF

175g (6oz) split red lentils

small thumb-sized piece of fresh ginger

1 fat garlic clove

1 teaspoon ground cumin

½–1 teaspoon turmeric

2 tablespoons peanut butter (chunky or smooth works fine)

juice of 1 lime

½–1 red or green chilli

naan, to serve (optional; leave this out to make it gluten free)

sea salt and freshly ground black pepper

FOR THE TARKA

1 red onion

small thumb-sized piece of fresh ginger

2 fat garlic cloves

200g (7oz) long-stem broccoli

3 tablespoons rapeseed or vegetable oil

2 tablespoons whole spices (I like a mix of cumin, coriander, mustard and onion seeds – use whatever you have)

200g (7oz) cherry tomatoes

1. Rinse the lentils in a sieve under cold water until the water turns clear, then tip into a saucepan. Finely grate in the ginger and garlic. Add the cumin, turmeric and a big pinch of salt, then pour in 700ml (24fl oz) water.
2. Put the pan over a high heat and bring to the boil, then reduce the heat to medium. Leave to simmer away, stirring occasionally, for 25–30 minutes, until the lentils are cooked through and most of the water has been absorbed.
3. Meanwhile, make the tarka. Finely slice the red onion, ginger and garlic cloves. Cut each broccoli piece in half, leaving you with a stalk and a head.
4. Heat 2 tablespoons of the oil in a frying pan over a medium heat. Add the onion and a pinch of salt. Cook for 5 minutes, stirring occasionally, until the onion has begun to soften, then add the broccoli and a splash of water to the pan (this helps the broccoli steam as it cooks).
5. Increase the heat to medium–high and fry for a further 3–4 minutes until the onion is soft and slightly caramelised. Add the whole spices, ginger and garlic, along with the remaining 1 tablespoon oil. Cook, stirring, for 1 minute more until the garlic is lightly golden, then add the whole cherry tomatoes.
6. Fry for a further 3–4 minutes until the broccoli is tender. Remove from the heat and season.
7. Come back to your dal, which will now be cooked. Stir through the peanut butter, then squeeze in the lime juice and season to taste. Finely slice the chilli.
8. Spoon the dal into two bowls. Top with the tomato and broccoli tarka, making sure to spoon over all the oil and spices, then scatter over the chilli, to serve. If extra hungry, eat with a naan.

Different Gears Greek Salad

In the summer, a Greek salad is one of the things I crave most. There's something about the combination of sweet tomatoes, salty feta and briny olives. When tomatoes are in season, I could pretty much live off them and bread, which got me thinking: why not add some fat oregano croutons into my favourite salad? Plus pickled onions. As Adam would say, different gears. Diane, sis, this is a bit of you.

Serves 2   Takes 20 minutes   V

1 small red onion

2–3 tablespoons red wine vinegar

pinch of caster (superfine) sugar (optional)

2 slices of sourdough (the noggins of a loaf of bread are perfect for this)

6 tablespoons extra virgin olive oil

2 teaspoons dried oregano, plus a sprinkle to serve

½ cucumber

3 ripe vine tomatoes

a large handful of mint

2 large handfuls of pitted olives (kalamata if you can get them; if not, use whatever is available)

100g (3½oz) feta

sea salt and freshly ground black pepper

1. Very finely slice the red onion. Scrape into a large salad bowl and pour over the red wine vinegar, then season well with salt, pepper and a pinch of sugar, if using. Use your hands to scrunch the onion into the vinegar – this will encourage it to soften and quickly pickle. Set aside.
2. Cut the bread into large croutons, then put into a bowl and toss with 1 tablespoon of the olive oil and the dried oregano. Season with salt.
3. Heat a frying pan over a medium–high heat. Add the croutons and fry, turning regularly, for around 5 minutes until golden and crisp. Set aside to cool slightly.
4. Slice the cucumber into half-moons, roughly chop the tomatoes and pick the mint leaves.
5. Pour the remaining 5 tablespoons olive oil into the bowl with the onions. Stir together to create your dressing. Add the cucumber, tomatoes, mint, olives and croutons, then crumble in the feta.
6. Give everything a brief toss to combine and coat in the pickled onion dressing. Taste for seasoning, adding a splash more vinegar if you like, then divide between two bowls and sprinkle over some more oregano, to serve.

Squash & Cauliflower Bulgur Bowl

If in doubt of what to cook, I always roast some veg, add a carb and make a green sauce to go with it. Here, the dressing is *mojo verde*, a punchy green sauce from the Canary Islands made with coriander, garlic, cumin and vinegar. With the harissa veg, grains and creamy yogurt, it's an epic combo.

Serves 2

Takes 35 minutes

V/VG/can be DF/can be GF (if using quinoa)

½ butternut squash

½ head of cauliflower

4½ tablespoons extra virgin olive oil

125g (4½oz) bulgur wheat (or, if you prefer quinoa or a bulgur/quinoa mix, use that instead)

50g (1¾oz) nuts of your choice, such as almonds or hazelnuts – I like a mixed bag (if you are nut-free, use mixed seeds instead)

2 teaspoons cumin seeds

1 small garlic clove

large handful of coriander (cilantro)

½–1 tablespoon sherry vinegar or white wine vinegar

1 heaped tablespoon harissa

2 large dollops of yogurt (natural, Greek or dairy free)

sea salt and freshly ground black pepper

1. Preheat your oven to 220°C/200°C fan/425°F/gas mark 7.
2. Chop the squash (leaving the skin on) into smallish cubes, then chop the cauliflower (stalk and all) into medium-sized pieces. Tip the squash and cauliflower pieces onto a large roasting tray. Toss with 1½ tablespoons of the oil and plenty of seasoning, then spread out into a single layer so they roast evenly. Roast for 25 minutes until cooked through and a little caramelised.
3. Meanwhile, cook the bulgur wheat or quinoa according to the packet instructions, then drain.
4. Toast the nuts in a small, dry frying pan over a medium heat until lightly golden. Tip into a bowl and leave to cool. Return the frying pan to the heat (no need to wash in between) and add the cumin seeds. Toast until they smell amazing, then tip into a small blender or small food processor.
5. Add the garlic, coriander, ½ tablespoon of the vinegar and the remaining 3 tablespoons extra virgin olive oil to the blender, along with a splash of water. Blitz everything together until smooth-ish – this is your mojo sauce. Season to taste, adding more vinegar if you think it needs it. If it's still a little thick, add a splash of water and blend again.
6. Roughly chop the toasted nuts and stir the harissa through the roasted vegetables.
7. Spread the yogurt across the bases of two bowls. Top with the bulgur, followed by the harissa veg, then drizzle over the green sauce and scatter over the nuts. Serve.

Roasted Garlic Veggie Caesar

Caesar salad is the GOAT, so of course I had to include one. My version includes roasted veg, lemony kale and roasted garlic to give incredible flavour to the dressing – plus croutons, OF COURSE. Anchovy-lover? It is, of course, legit to blitz as many as you like into the dressing.

Serves 2   Takes 30 minutes   V

1 large sweet potato or ½ butternut squash

1 red onion

2 tablespoons olive oil

4 fat garlic cloves

2 large slices of crusty bread

2 handfuls of kale

juice of ½ lemon (use the other half in the dressing below)

1 chicory (witlof) or small radicchio (I like the pink ones because they are beaut!)

sea salt and freshly ground black pepper

FOR THE DRESSING

30g (1oz) vegetarian parmesan, plus extra to serve

2 egg yolks (save the whites for Pops's Seeded Granola on page 197)

1 teaspoon Dijon mustard

juice of ½ lemon

3 tablespoons extra virgin olive oil

1. Preheat your oven to 220°C/200°C fan/425°F/gas mark 7.
2. Leaving the skin on, cut the sweet potato or squash into medium-sized chunks. Cut the onion into 8 wedges. Toss the sweet potato or squash and onion in a roasting tray with 1 tablespoon of the olive oil and plenty of seasoning, then spread into a single layer so the veg cooks evenly. Wrap the garlic cloves in foil (leaving the skin on) and place on the tray. Roast for 20–25 minutes until the veg are soft and a little caramelised.
3. Cut the bread into large croutons. Place on a second roasting tray, and drizzle with the remaining 1 tablespoon oil. Season well, then roast for 8–12 minutes until golden and crisp, flipping halfway. Set aside to cool.
4. Meanwhile, put the kale into a large bowl. Squeeze in the lemon juice and season with a big pinch of salt, then use your hands to scrunch the lemon juice into the kale – this will help it soften. Separate the chicory or radicchio leaves, add these to the bowl too.
5. For the dressing, finely grate the cheese. Put into a blender or small food processor, along with the egg yolks, mustard, lemon juice and olive oil. Blitz to form a smooth, creamy dressing.
6. Unwrap the foil parcel of garlic and squeeze the cooked garlic cloves into the dressing, then blitz again to combine. Season to taste with salt and lots of black pepper. The dressing will be lacking a little acidity at this stage, but don't worry, because you're mixing it with the lemony kale!
7. Scrape the roasted veg into the bowl with the kale mix, then add the croutons and most of the dressing. Gently toss everything together to coat in the dressing, then divide between two plates. Drizzle the remaining dressing over each plate and serve with the extra cheese grated over as you like.

Braised Butterbeans with Herby Yogurt

You can't beat a one-pot dish full of warming spice and greens. Beans are always what I go to when I want some quick and easy veg-packed comfort food. Here, I've added a herby lemon and cumin yogurt for some added zippy freshness. Enjoy.

Serves 2 | Takes 30 minutes | V/can be VG/can be DF/GF

1 tablespoon cumin seeds

1 red onion

2 tablespoons olive oil

4 fat garlic cloves

robust greens of your choice – either ½ sliced cabbage (any green variety will be great) or 1 sliced cavolo nero or 100g (3½oz) sliced kale

300ml (10½fl oz) vegetable stock

2 teaspoons smoked paprika

150ml (5fl oz) white wine

660g (1lb 7oz) jar of butterbeans or 2 × 400g (14oz) tins (this recipe is all about the beans, so it's worth splashing out on a jar if you can; I've become obsessed with Bold Beans)

large handful of parsley and/or coriander (cilantro)

150g (5½oz) natural or Greek yogurt (use non-dairy yogurt to make it vegan or dairy free)

zest and juice of ½ lemon

sea salt and freshly ground black pepper

1. Toast the cumin seeds in a medium saucepan (one large enough to cook the beans in later) over a medium heat until smelling amazing, then tip into a bowl.
2. Finely chop the red onion. Scrape into the same saucepan, along with the olive oil and a pinch of salt. Cook over a medium heat, stirring occasionally, for 8–10 minutes, until softened but not coloured.
3. Meanwhile, finely slice the garlic cloves and the greens if they need it. Make up your vegetable stock.
4. Add the garlic to the onion and cook, stirring, for 1 minute more, then add three-quarters of the toasted cumin seeds, along with the smoked paprika. Stir everything together, then pour in the white wine. Once the wine has bubbled away by half, tip in the butterbeans, along with all their juices from the can or jar, and pour in the stock. Stir, then leave to simmer away for 5–10 minutes, depending on the quality and softness of your beans.
5. While the beans are braising make the yogurt. In a blender or small food processor, combine the remaining cumin seeds with most of the herbs (stalks and all), along with the yogurt, and the lemon zest and juice. Blitz until green, then season to taste.
6. Come back to the beans: add the greens and cook for around 5 minutes until nicely wilted. Season the beans to taste.
7. Ladle the beans and their sauce into two serving bowls. Drizzle over the green yogurt, then scatter over the remaining herbs, to serve.

Fish with Lentils & Sauce Vierge

Sauce vierge is a warm French tomato salsa. It sounds fancy; in fact, it's super easy to make. I've added olives and coriander seeds for a kick that is unreal with pan-fried fish. This dish will reset you for the week ahead while being casually very impressive, perfect for when you want to feel like a kitchen don.

Serves 2   Takes 30 minutes   DF/GF

1 teaspoon coriander seeds

200g (7oz) cherry tomatoes

2 handfuls of olives (I like black kalamata olives best here)

handful of basil

zest and juice of 1 lemon

1 garlic clove

5 tablespoons extra virgin olive oil

2 large handfuls of spinach

250g (9oz) pre-cooked puy or green lentils pouch (or you can use a 400g/14oz tin, drained)

2 firm white fish fillets (I like hake or haddock), skin on

sea salt and freshly ground black pepper

1. Toast the coriander seeds in a small, dry frying pan over a medium heat. Tip the seeds into a pestle and mortar, along with a pinch of salt, then roughly grind.
2. Roughly dice the cherry tomatoes and olives. Finely slice the basil stalks, keeping the leaves whole.
3. Return the ground coriander seeds to the small frying pan (off the heat). Add the tomatoes, olives, basil stalks and lemon zest. Finely grate the garlic into the pan. Pour over 4 tablespoons of the extra virgin olive oil. Stir, then set aside your sauce vierge.
4. Add the spinach and lentils to a medium-sized saucepan, along with a big splash of water. Season and place over a low–medium heat. Cook, stirring occasionally, until the spinach has wilted and the lentils are warm.
5. Meanwhile, pat the fish dry with paper towels and season well on both sides with salt and pepper.
6. Place a non-stick frying pan over a high heat. Once the pan is visibly hot, pour in the remaining 1 tablespoon olive oil and add the fish, skin-side down. Once the fish hits the hot pan, it will begin to curl, so use a fish slice to press down on it while it cooks – this is the secret to crispy skin.
7. Fry the fish skin-side down until the edges turn white (you want it to be two-thirds cooked before you flip it over). This will take 2–4 minutes, depending on thickness.
8. Flip the fish so it's skin-side up, then reduce the heat to low and cook for a further 1–2 minutes until cooked to your liking.
9. Once you've flipped the fish, gently warm through the sauce vierge. Stir through the basil leaves and season with salt, pepper and lemon juice to taste.
10. Divide the spinach and lentils between two plates. Top each with a piece of fish, then spoon over the sauce to serve.

Sunday

Feasts

Urfa Chilli Roast Chicken with Cumin & Sumac New Potato Salad + Asparagus with Warm Chilli Dressing

① + ② + ③

Serves 6 | Takes 1 hour 30 minutes | can be DF/GF

Urfa Chilli Roast Chicken

1.6–1.8kg (3lb 8oz–4lb) whole chicken (get the best quality you can afford – it makes all the difference to the flavour!)

2 extra chicken legs (optional, but a good idea if you know you're feeding hungry people!)

2 tablespoons olive oil

3–4 tablespoons urfa chilli paste (or rose harissa if you can't get it)

300g (10½oz) Greek yogurt (optional; leave this out to make it dairy free)

handful of dill

sea salt and freshly ground black pepper

1. Preheat your oven to 220°C/200°C fan/425°F/gas mark 7.
2. Place the chicken on a chopping board, breast-side down. Starting at the tail end, use a pair of sharp, clean kitchen scissors to cut down both sides of the back bone to remove it. Now turn the chicken over so that it's breast-side up. Using a sharp knife, cut the legs and wings away from the main body of the chicken – with the back bone removed it will be easy to see where the joints are. When you are finished, you'll have 2 legs, 2 wings and a chicken crown. Prepping your bird like this will give you the most even, juicy cooked chook!
3. Put the chicken legs (along with the extras, if using) and wings into a large roasting tray. Drizzle with 1 tablespoon of the olive oil and season liberally. Roast for 20 minutes.
4. After 20 minutes, add the crown to the roasting tray. Drizzle with the remaining 1 tablespoon oil and season super well. Roast for a further 20–25 minutes until all the chicken is cooked through, juicy and tender. If you have a thermometer, you want the chicken crown's internal temperature to read 75°C (167°F). If not, just make sure the juices are running clear.
5. Transfer the chicken to a board to rest for 15 minutes. Keep the roasting tray with the chicken juices warm in a low oven.
6. Once the chicken has rested, use two forks to shred the leg meat from the bones, and return this meat to the roasting tray. Add the urfa chilli paste and mix well to combine.
7. Meanwhile, cut the breasts away from the crown and slice.
8. Spread the yogurt, if using, onto a large platter. Top with the spicy leg meat, crispy wings and juicy breast meat. Roughly chop the dill and scatter over to serve, along with a good pinch of sea salt. Game-changer – you'll never roast your chicken in any other way.

Cumin & Sumac New Potato Salad

1.2kg (2lb 10oz) new potatoes

2 tablespoons cumin seeds

2 teaspoons sumac

1 teaspoon chilli flakes
(optional)

2 teaspoons honey or maple
syrup (use maple syrup to
make it vegan)

1½ lemons (use the other half
for the asparagus below)

6 tablespoons extra
virgin olive oil

large handful of parsley,
chives or coriander (cilantro),
or a mixture of all three

sea salt and freshly ground
black pepper

1. Cut the potatoes in half or into quarters, depending on their size. Put into a large saucepan, cover with cold water and season well. Bring to the boil. Once boiling, cook for 10–15 minutes until tender. Drain and leave to steam for a few minutes.
2. Meanwhile, make the dressing. Toast the cumin seeds in a small dry frying pan over a medium heat until smelling amazing. Tip into a pestle and mortar, along with a pinch of salt, and roughly crush (or leave them whole if you prefer).
3. Tip the toasted cumin into a large serving bowl. Add the sumac, chilli flakes (if using) and honey or maple syrup. Zest and squeeze in the lemons and add the olive oil. Stir and season well. The dressing should be super zesty and sharp – the potatoes will absorb it and taste banging!
4. Tip the steamed potatoes into the dressing, toss to combine and leave for a bit to let the flavours mingle. (If making in advance, cover and refrigerate overnight at this point; just bring to room temperature before serving the next day.)
5. When ready to serve, roughly chop the herbs (stalks and all) and mix through, giving everything one last season to taste.

Asparagus with Warm Chilli Dressing

50g (1¾oz) mixed seeds

2 teaspoons honey
or maple syrup

1 teaspoon smoked paprika

4 fat garlic cloves

1–2 red chillies

2 tablespoons olive oil

750g (1lb 10oz) asparagus
spears

juice of ½ lemon

sea salt

1. Toast the seeds in a small dry frying pan over a medium heat until starting to pop. Add the honey or maple syrup and smoked paprika, along with a good pinch of salt. Cook, stirring, for a further 30 seconds, until sticky and caramelised, then scrape out onto a piece of baking paper and leave to cool. Once cool, break the mixture into pieces.
2. Finely slice the garlic and chilli, then add to a small frying pan, along with the olive oil. Cook over a medium heat for 2–3 minutes, stirring regularly, until everything is soft and the garlic is lightly golden. Remove from the heat.
3. Snap or trim the ends off your asparagus, then cook in salted boiling water in a large saucepan for 1–2 minutes until vivid green and tender. Drain, then tip onto a platter.
4. Reheat the garlic and chilli dressing and squeeze in the lemon juice. Pour the dressing over the asparagus, and top with the honeyed seeds and a sprinkling of salt, to serve. YUM.

②

③

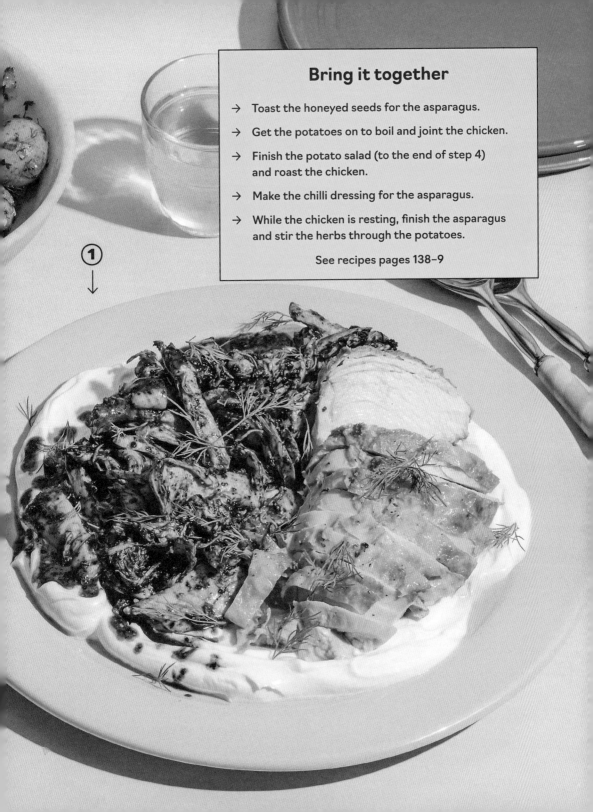

Bring it together

→ Toast the honeyed seeds for the asparagus.

→ Get the potatoes on to boil and joint the chicken.

→ Finish the potato salad (to the end of step 4) and roast the chicken.

→ Make the chilli dressing for the asparagus.

→ While the chicken is resting, finish the asparagus and stir the herbs through the potatoes.

See recipes pages 138–9

① ↓

Battered Fish Tacos with Salsa Macha Slaw + Orange & Tomato Salsa

Serves 6　　　　　Takes 1 hour 30 minutes　　　　　can be GF

175g (6oz) plain (all-purpose) flour (use gluten-free flour to make it gluten free)

75g (2¾oz) cornflour (cornstarch)

1 teaspoon baking powder

1 tablespoon ground cumin

1 tablespoon ground coriander

2 teaspoons smoked paprika

1 teaspoon chilli powder

1kg (2lb 4oz) skinless, boneless, firm white fish (I like hake, cod or haddock)

18 small tortillas (use corn tortillas to make it gluten free)

light rapeseed, vegetable or sunflower oil, for frying

330ml (11¼oz) cold beer or sparkling water (pale ale or lager work best; use a gluten-free beer or sparkling water to make it gluten free)

lime wedges, to serve

sea salt and freshly ground black pepper

FOR THE PICKLED ONION

1 red onion

juice of 1 lime

Battered Fish Tacos

1.　To make the pickle, very finely slice the red onion and scrape into a small bowl with the lime juice. Season with a good pinch of salt. Scrunch the onion into the lime juice – this will encourage it to soften and quickly pickle. Set aside.

2.　For the chipotle yogurt, mix the ingredients together in a second small bowl, season to taste and set aside.

3.　Measure the flour, cornflour, baking powder and spices into a large bowl. Season well and stir together.

4.　Pat the fish dry with paper towels, then cut into roughly bite-sized pieces. Season.

5.　Heat a large, high-sided frying pan over a high heat. Fry the tortillas until they are a little charred in places, then wrap them in a clean tea towel or inside some foil to keep warm.

6.　Pour the oil into the same frying pan to a depth of 2.5cm (1 inch). Heat over a medium–high heat until the oil is visibly shimmering; if you have a digital thermometer, you want it to be 180°C (350°F). If you don't have a thermometer, you can drop a small piece of tortilla into the oil to test the heat; it should brown in 20 seconds.

7.　While the oil is heating, pour the beer or water into the spiced flour mix and whisk until you have a thin, smooth batter. Line a roasting tray with paper towels.

8.　Working in batches, dunk the fish pieces into the batter, then carefully lower into the oil. Fry, turning halfway, for around 1–2 minutes until crisp and golden, and the fish is cooked through. Using a slotted spoon, transfer to the paper-towel-lined tray and sprinkle with salt. Repeat until all the fish has been fried.

FOR THE CHIPOTLE YOGURT

3–4 teaspoons chipotle paste
(depending on how spicy you
like it)

300g (10½oz) Greek yogurt

A digital thermometer will
make life very easy here

9. Serve the fish tacos with the lime wedges, tortillas, chipotle yogurt and pickled onions, along with the recipes below for a true taco feast.

Tip: If you've got any leftover fish, it actually reheats super well. Line a baking tray with baking paper, then bake the fish in the oven at 220°C/200°C fan/425°F/gas mark 7 for 10 minutes.

---

②

1 small red cabbage

½ bunch of spring onions
(scallions) – use the rest in the
Orange & Tomato Salsa below

large handful of
coriander (cilantro)

zest and juice of 2 limes

6–8 tablespoons Salsa Macha
(page 193)

sea salt and freshly ground
black pepper

Salsa Macha Slaw

1. Very finely slice the red cabbage and spring onions (both green and white parts). Roughly chop the coriander (stalks and all). Combine the cabbage, spring onions and coriander in a large bowl.
2. Add the lime zest and juice, followed by the salsa macha.
3. Toss the slaw with your hands so it gets coated in the dressing and season to taste. (This will happily sit for a few hours.)

Tip: No salsa macha? Don't worry! Simply dress all the slaw ingredients with 4 teaspoons chipotle paste, 4 tablespoons olive oil, 50g (1¾oz) toasted mixed seeds and the juice of 2 limes.

---

2 oranges

400g (14oz) cherry tomatoes

½ bunch of spring onions
(scallions)

1 green or red chilli

1 teaspoon ground cumin

1 teaspoon ground coriander

1 garlic clove

juice of 1 lime

sea salt and freshly ground
black pepper

Orange & Tomato Salsa

1. Segment the oranges over a bowl so you can catch the juice, then squeeze the skin so you get all the remaining juice into the bowl. Once segmented, chop the oranges into smallish pieces, then add these to the bowl with the juice.
2. Cut the tomatoes into quarters. Add these to the bowl too. Very finely slice the spring onions (both green and white parts). Finely chop the chilli, and add both to the salsa.
3. Add the spices, then finely grate in the garlic. Add the lime juice. Stir and season to taste. (This can be prepared 1 hour before serving.)

Bring it together

→ Make the Salsa Macha, if using (page 193).

→ Make the slaw.

→ Pickle the red onions and make the chipotle yogurt.

→ Make the tomato salsa.

→ Heat the tortillas, and batter and fry the fish for the tacos.

See recipes pages 142–3

①

Spiced Cauliflower with Muhammara, Charred Baby Gem with Green Tahini + Zhoug Grains

 + ② + ③

Serves 6   Takes 2 hours   V/VG/DF/can be GF

2 cauliflowers

2 tablespoons Middle Eastern-style spice mix (such as ras el hanout or Lebanese 7 spice)

3 tablespoons olive oil, plus extra to serve

small handful of mixed herbs (I love dill, parsley or mint)

sea salt and freshly ground black pepper

FOR THE MUHAMMARA

150g (5½oz) walnuts

4 roasted red peppers from a jar, drained

½ teaspoon smoked paprika

½ teaspoon Middle Eastern-style spice mix

1 teaspoon Aleppo chilli or ½ teaspoon dried chilli flakes, plus extra to serve

2 tablespoons pomegranate molasses, plus extra to serve

2 tablespoons olive oil

Tip: The dressings can be made a day in advance and kept in the fridge. The dukkah can be made a month in advance.

Spiced Cauliflower with Muhammara

1. Preheat your oven to 180°C/160°C fan/350°F/gas mark 4.
2. For the muhammara, roast the walnuts on a roasting tray for 5–8 minutes until nicely golden, then leave to cool. Tip into a blender or small food processor with the remaining ingredients, then blitz until smooth. Season to taste, then set aside.
3. Increase the oven temperature to 220°C/200°C fan/425°F/gas mark 7.
4. Cut each cauliflower into 6 large wedges, leaving a few of the smaller leaves attached. Put onto a large roasting tray (use 2 if that's easier). Rub all over with the spice mix, then season and drizzle with the olive oil. Roast for 25–30 minutes until cooked through and nicely charred.
5. Roughly chop the herbs.
6. Once the cauliflower is cooked, spread the muhammara across the base of a large serving platter. Lay the cauliflower on top, then drizzle with a little more olive oil and pomegranate molasses. Scatter over the herbs and sprinkle over a little more chilli. Eat with the charred Baby Gems and Zhoug Grains opposite. YESSS.

2 spring onions (scallions)

large handful of mixed herbs

4 tablespoons tahini

zest and juice of 1 lemon

3 Baby Gem lettuces

1 tablespoon olive oil

handful of pomegranate seeds

sea salt

FOR THE DUKKHA

2 teaspoons each of cumin
seeds and coriander seeds

2 tablespoons sesame seeds

50g (1¾oz) toasted walnuts

big pinch of Aleppo chilli
or chilli flakes (optional)

200g (7oz) dried grains
of your choice

200g (7oz) fine green beans

250g (9oz) frozen peas

sea salt and freshly ground
black pepper

FOR THE ZHOUG

½–1 green chilli

about 100g (3½oz) coriander
(cilantro)

1 fat garlic clove

2 teaspoons each toasted
cumin and coriander seeds

juice of 1½ lemons

6 tablespoons olive oil

pinch of caster (superfine)
sugar (optional)

Charred Baby Gem with Green Tahini

1. To make the dukkha, toast the cumin and coriander seeds in a dry frying pan over a medium heat until smelling amazing, then tip into a pestle and mortar or spice grinder and roughly grind. Transfer into a small bowl.
2. Toast the sesame seeds in the same pan, then add to the bowl. Chop the walnuts and add these to the bowl too. Season everything with a big pinch of salt and chilli, if using.
3. Roughly chop the spring onions. Put into a blender or small food processor. Add the herbs, tahini, lemon zest and juice, and 4 tablespoons water. Blitz to a vivid green drizzle-able dressing, adding more water if needed. Season to taste.
4. Place a large frying pan or griddle pan over a super-high heat. Meanwhile, cut the Baby Gems in half. Season and drizzle with the olive oil, then place them in the hot pan, cut-sides down. Fry for 2–3 minutes until the undersides are nicely charred, then transfer to a serving plate.
5. Spoon the dressing over the Baby Gems, then scatter over the pomegranate seeds and dukkha to serve.

Zhoug Grains

1. Make the zhoug. Roughly chop the chilli, then put into a blender or small food processor along with the coriander (stalks and all), garlic clove and toasted spices. Add the lemon juice, olive oil and 2 tablespoons water. Blitz until you have a smooth green sauce – if your blender is quite small, add the coriander in stages. Season with salt and pepper and, if it needs it, add sugar to taste. Set aside.
2. Cook your grain of choice according to the packet instructions.
3. Meanwhile, put a saucepan of salted water on to boil. Trim the green beans, if needed, then, once the water's boiling, cook for 2 minutes. Add the peas and cook for 1 minute more. Drain and rinse until cool, then tip into a large bowl.
4. Add the cooked grains to the greens, then stir through the zhoug. Season everything to taste. This can be done a few hours in advance.

Bring it together

→ Toast all the walnuts and cumin/coriander seeds for all recipes.

→ Make the dukkha.

→ Make the muhammara, the green tahini dressing and the zhoug.

→ Finish the zhoug grains and roast the cauliflower.

→ Char the Baby Gems and pile everything on to platters.

See recipes pages 146–7

③

② →

'Nduja King Prawns with Confit Tomato Orzo + Fried Courgettes with Marinated Feta

Serves 6

Takes 2 hours

'Nduja King Prawns

5 tablespoons olive oil
(or confit tomato oil from
the Confit Tomato Orzo
below)

150g (5½oz) 'nduja

18 shell-on king prawns

focaccia, to serve (optional
if extra hungry)

sea salt and freshly ground
black pepper

1. Heat 1 tablespoon of oil in a large saucepan over a medium heat. Add the 'nduja and cook until 'melted' and beginning to crisp, using the back of your spoon to smoosh it into small pieces. Once cooked, take off the heat and set aside.
2. Pat dry the king prawns with paper towels then season well with salt and pepper. Heat a large non-stick frying pan over a high heat until searingly hot. Add 2 tablespoons of oil, then fry half the prawns for 2–3 minutes until they have turned from grey to completely pink and are a little charred in places. Once cooked, tip into the pan of 'nduja and repeat with the remaining prawns and oil.
3. Place the pan of cooked prawns and 'nduja over a low heat and gently reheat, tossing the prawns so each one gets completely coated. Serve with the recipes below, plus some focaccia, if you like.

Confit Tomato Orzo

1 fat garlic bulb

800g (1lb 12oz) cherry
tomatoes on the vine

a few sprigs of thyme

½–1 teaspoon chilli flakes

about 300ml (10½fl oz) olive
oil (don't worry, you won't be
eating it all!)

1. Preheat your oven to 160°C/140°C fan/325°F/gas mark 3.
2. Separate the garlic cloves (keeping their skin on) and take all the cherry tomatoes off the vine – it will be a real faff if you try to do it later.
3. Tightly pack the garlic cloves and tomatoes into a medium-sized roasting tin. Add the thyme and chilli flakes, then pour over enough olive oil to cover the bottom half of the tomatoes. Season well, then cover with foil and roast for 50 minutes–1 hour, or until the tomatoes are just bursting and the garlic is soft. Leave to cool slightly, then separate the tomatoes and garlic from the oil, keeping both (this can be done the day before).

350g (12oz) orzo

2 roasted red peppers
from a jar

small bunch each
of parsley and basil

sea salt and freshly ground
black pepper

4. Pour 700ml (24fl oz) boiling water into a large saucepan. Season well with salt, then drop in the orzo. Cook for 8 minutes until the orzo is just cooked and you are left with around 100ml (3½fl oz) pasta water, which will be used for your sauce. Set aside.

5. Meanwhile, squeeze the cooked garlic cloves from their skins and place in a blender or small food processor. Add the roasted red peppers and a good splash of the tomato oil, then blitz until smooth. Roughly chop the parsley and basil (stalks and all).

6. Once the orzo is cooked, stir through the whole confit cherry tomatoes and the red pepper purée. Cook gently to heat through, stir in most of the chopped herbs, then season to taste with salt, pepper and more of the confit tomato oil.

7. Spoon into a large serving bowl, then top with the remaining herbs and some cracked black pepper. Serve.

200g (7oz) feta

½ teaspoon chilli flakes

1 teaspoon sumac (optional, but adds a real zesty kick)

2 tablespoons olive oil, plus extra for drizzling

50g (1¾oz) sunflower seeds

3 large courgettes (zucchinis)

zest and juice of 1 lemon or 2 tablespoons white wine vinegar

4 tablespoons capers

sea salt and freshly ground black pepper

*

Tip: The feta and sunflower seeds can be prepared up to a day in advance.

Fried Courgettes with Marinated Feta

1. Crumble the feta into medium chunks in a small bowl. Sprinkle over the chilli flakes and sumac, if using, then pour over a good drizzle of olive oil. Stir to just coat each piece of feta, then set aside in the fridge to marinate.

2. Toast the sunflower seeds in a small, dry frying pan over a medium heat until golden. Season and tip into a small bowl, then leave to cool.

3. Cut the courgettes into thick half-moons. Put these into a large bowl, and toss with the olive oil. Season with salt and pepper.

4. Heat a large, non-stick frying pan over a high heat. Fry the courgettes, working in batches, for around 2 minutes on each side until tender and nicely browned. Tip onto a serving plate. Once all the courgettes are fried, scatter over the lemon zest and juice, or drizzle over the white wine vinegar.

5. Top the courgettes with the capers, followed by the marinated feta and toasted sunflower seeds. This salad is best served at room temperature.

Bring it together

→ Marinate the feta and toast the sunflower seeds for the courgettes.

→ Confit the tomatoes for the orzo.

→ Finish the courgette salad.

→ Melt the 'nduja and finish the tomato confit orzo.

→ Fry the prawns and serve.

See recipes pages 150–1

② →

Anchovy & Leek Bean Gratin, Broccoli with Charred Lemon Dressing + Shaved Fennel Salad

Serves 6   Takes 1 hour 20 minutes   can be GF

3 leeks, washed

100g (3½oz) jar
of anchovies in oil

8 fat garlic cloves

handful of thyme sprigs
or fresh oregano

2 × 660g (1lb 7oz) jars
butterbeans or 4 × 400g
(14oz) tins

2–3 teaspoons fennel seeds
(I like 3 – you do you)

250ml (9fl oz) white wine

300ml (10½fl oz) double
(heavy) cream

100g (3½oz) parmesan
or pecorino cheese

30g (1oz) panko or gluten-
free breadcrumbs (if GF)

zest of 2 lemons (use the
zested lemons in the broccoli
salad below)

sea salt and freshly ground
black pepper

*

Tip: This can be prepared a
few hours in advance up to the
end of step 6. Just leave the
beans in the saucepan, covered
with a lid. When ready to serve,
gently reheat and follow the
instructions for grilling.

Anchovy & Leek Bean Gratin

1. Halve the leeks lengthways, then finely slice into half-moons. Scrape into your largest saucepan. Add the oil from the anchovy jar and a pinch of salt, then cook over a medium heat, stirring occasionally, for 8–10 minutes until collapsed and softened.

2. Meanwhile, finely chop the garlic cloves (or finely grate them, if you find it easier). Strip the thyme from their sprigs, or chop the oregano if using. Drain the butterbeans through a sieve.

3. Return to the leeks. Add the anchovies to the pan, along with the garlic, fennel seeds and herbs. Cook, smooshing the anchovies with the back of your spoon, until they have 'melted' into the leeks, then pour in the white wine.

4. Once the wine has bubbled away for a couple of minutes, tip in the butterbeans and pour in the cream. Give everything a good mix to combine. Let the beans bubble, still over a medium heat, for around 10 minutes until you have a slightly thickened, creamy stew. You want the sauce to cling to the beans; bear in mind that it won't thicken under the grill, so get it to your preferred consistency at this stage.

5. While the beans are bubbling, finely grate the cheese. Mix half with the breadcrumbs and a good crack of black pepper.

6. Stir the lemon zest into the beans, along with the remaining cheese. Once melted, season to taste.

7. Preheat your grill to medium.

8. Decant the warm stew into an ovenproof baking dish. Top with the cheesy breadcrumbs, then slide under the grill for 5 minutes or until the top is golden.

9. Leave to sit for a few minutes before serving with the broccoli and fennel salad, opposite.

Broccoli with Charred Lemon Dressing

2 lemons

1 teaspoon smoked paprika

2–3 teaspoons honey or maple syrup (use maple syrup to make it vegan)

7 tablespoons olive oil

600g (1lb 5oz) purple sprouting or long-stem broccoli

handful of thyme sprigs or fresh oregano (use the same herbs you used for the gratin)

sea salt and freshly ground black pepper

1. For the charred lemon dressing, heat a frying pan over a high heat. Cut the lemons in half and place them, cut-side down, into the pan. Fry for 3–4 minutes until the undersides are blackened, then take off the heat and leave to cool slightly.
2. Once cool enough to handle, squeeze the juice from the lemons into a bowl (they should be super jammy). Add the smoked paprika, honey or maple syrup and 5 tablespoons of the olive oil. Stir and season the dressing to taste.
3. Bring a large saucepan of salted water to the boil. Cut the broccoli pieces in half lengthways.
4. Once the water is boiling, drop in the broccoli and cook for 2 minutes (depending on the size of your pan, you may need to do this in batches), then drain and leave to cool. If you have a wire rack, spread out the cooked broccoli on the rack to cool – this will help it steam dry and stay super green.
5. When you're ready to eat, heat a large frying pan over a super-high heat – you want it raging. Working in batches, drizzle the broccoli with the remaining 2 tablespoons olive oil, season well, then lay cut-side down in the pan. Fry for 2–3 minutes until the underside is nicely charred, then transfer to a serving platter. Repeat with all the broccoli.
6. Pour the dressing over the hot broccoli, then strip the herbs off their sprigs and scatter over the top, to serve. Banging.

Tip: The dressing can be made the day before and kept in the fridge. You can also blanch the broccoli the day before; once cool, just pop it in the fridge.

Shaved Fennel Salad

50g (1¾oz) sunflower seeds, or pumpkin seeds (pepitas)

big pinch of chilli flakes

2 large fennel bulbs

large handful of parsley

4 tablespoons capers

1 lemon

2 tablespoons olive oil

sea salt and freshly ground black pepper

1. Toast the seeds in a dry frying pan over a medium heat until nicely golden, then tip into a small bowl, add the chilli flakes and season.
2. Pick the fennel fronds off the fennel and set them aside for later. Next, using a sharp knife (or a mandoline if you find that easier), very finely slice the fennel bulbs.
3. Put the sliced fennel into a large serving bowl. Roughly chop the parsley (stalks and all) and add to the bowl, along with the capers and chilli seeds. Zest and juice in the lemon, then add the olive oil and mix everything to combine.
4. Season to taste and scatter over the fennel fronds, to serve.

1 →

② ③

Bring it together

→ Toast the sunflower seeds for the
  fennel salad.

→ Make the charred lemon dressing
  and blanch the broccoli.

→ Make the gratin.

→ Finish the fennel salad.

→ Grill the gratin and char the broccoli.

See recipes pages 154–5

Sunday

⑥

Sweets!

Ode to Kinder Chocolate Cake

This cake is crack. People who know me, can attest that I LOVE chocolate and cake; in fact, over the years, I have written many a recipe for a chocolate cake, and this is my best yet. It's soft and fudgey without being dense. And don't even get me started on the chocolate hazelnut icing; it's so light and moreish. A thing of beauty.

Serves 12

Takes 1 hour 20 minutes   V

185g (6½oz) soft salted butter, plus extra for greasing

150g (5½oz) dark chocolate

240g (8½oz) soft brown sugar

150g (5½oz) self-raising flour

2 tablespoons cocoa powder

¾ teaspoon bicarbonate soda (baking soda)

¼ teaspoon fine sea salt

225g (8oz) natural yogurt or soured cream

3 medium eggs

50ml (2fl oz) boiling water

handful of toasted hazelnuts, to serve (optional)

Kinder Buenos (as many as you want; I like to use a mixture of milk chocolate and white chocolate)

1. Preheat your oven to 180°C/160°C fan/350°F/gas mark 4. Grease a 20 × 20cm (8 × 8 inch) brownie tin with a smidge of butter, then line with baking paper.
2. Place the butter into a heatproof bowl. Snap in the dark chocolate. Melt together in the microwave on high, heating in 30-second bursts and stirring until melted. Alternatively, place the bowl over a pan of just simmering water and stir until melted. Leave to cool slightly.
3. In a large bowl, whisk together the soft brown sugar, flour, cocoa powder, bicarb and salt until there are no lumps of sugar.
4. In a separate bowl, whisk together the yogurt or soured cream with the eggs until roughly combined. Don't worry if it looks a little lumpy – that's normal!
5. Pour the egg mixture into the dry ingredients, then scrape in the melted chocolate and butter. Whisk everything together until a smooth cake batter forms, then pour in the boiling water and whisk again – this is the secret to a fudgey chocolate cake!
6. Pour the batter into your lined tin and bake in the centre of the oven for 35–40 minutes until the cake is well risen and a skewer (or piece of spaghetti!) poked into the centre comes out clean, or with a few dry crumbs attached.
7. Leave to cool for 10 minutes in its tin, then remove from the tin and transfer to a wire rack to cool completely.
8. Now for the most incredibly delicious Swiss meringue buttercream. Place the egg whites in a heatproof bowl, along with the caster sugar. Place over a small saucepan of barely simmering water set over a low heat. Whisk the egg whites and sugar together until the sugar has dissolved and the mixture has turned opaque and super white.

FOR THE SWISS MERINGUE BUTTERCREAM

2 medium egg whites (save the yolks and use them in the Roasted Garlic Veggie Caesar on page 130 or my Cardamom Crème Brûlée on page 168)

100g (3½oz) caster (superfine) sugar

200g (7oz) soft butter

6–8 tablespoons Nutella or any chocolate and hazelnut spread (depending on how much you love it – this is a party cake!)

pinch of fine sea salt

9. Take the bowl off the heat. Using an electric whisk, keep whisking until the egg whites and sugar have turned into a stiff-peak-stage meringue. Now, while still whisking, gradually add the butter. It will melt into the egg whites and sugar, turning the mixture into a super-shiny buttercream with the texture of just-whipped cream (see below for tips).

10. Whisk in the Nutella, along with a pinch of salt. Taste, and cry tears of joy.

11. Spread the icing all over the top of the cake. Roughly chop the toasted hazelnuts, if using, then break over the Kinder Buenos and sprinkle with the nuts to serve. Ridiculous.

↓

A couple of tips for making Swiss meringue buttercream
If you melt the butter into the icing and it turns super thin, don't panic! It just means your buttercream is a bit warm. Pop the bowl into the fridge for 15 minutes, then re-whisk to bring it back to life!

If the buttercream looks grainy, don't panic! It just means your buttercream is a bit cold. Place back over a pan of barely simmering water and whisk to re-melt the butter, and it will be grand.

Tip: The cake can be baked the day before icing and then well wrapped. Once iced, the cake will happily keep in an airtight container at room temperature for up to 3 days.

**Ode to Kinder
Chocolate Cake**

↓

page 160

Peach, Honey & Yogurt Pavlova

My favourite thing about working in professional kitchens is the knowledge shared between chefs. This pavlova is a case in point: my chef pal told me to add all the sugar to the egg whites in the beginning, and then whisk. Trust me, it really works, and actually creates a more stable pav – which, paired with the yogurt and honey, is truly outrageous. Thank you to Bex Song for the tip!

Serves 4–6   Takes 2 hours 10 minutes   V/GF

4 medium egg whites (you want 140–150g/5–5½oz egg white altogether) – save the yolks and use them in the Roasted Garlic Veggie Caesar (page 130) and/or Cardamom Crème Brûlée (page 168)

280–300g (10–10½oz) caster (superfine) sugar

150ml (5fl oz) double (heavy) cream

300g (10½oz) Greek yogurt

2–3 tablespoons honey, plus a drizzle to serve

3 peaches (or use apricots/ nectarines if you can't get them)

handful of shelled pistachios

*

Tip: The pavlova can be baked a couple of days before. Once it's completely cool, keep it airtight – either in a container or wrapped well on the tray in clingfilm, at room temperature.

1. Preheat your oven to 120°C/100°C fan/235°F/gas mark ½. Line a large baking tray with baking paper.
2. Weigh your egg whites into a bowl, then measure in double the amount of sugar.
3. Using an electric whisk or stand mixer, whisk the egg whites and sugar together until they form a shiny meringue that holds its shape. This will take around 10 minutes. When it's ready, you should be able to lift the bowl upside down over your head without it pouring all over you! I start whisking on a slower speed and then, once the eggs and sugar have combined and turned an opaque white, I increase the speed.
4. Use a little bit of your meringue to stick the baking paper to the tray, then, using a metal spoon, dollop the rest of the meringue into the centre of the tray to create your pavlova. Use the back of the spoon to create a divot in the centre of the meringue. If you like your meringue to look fancy, you can then use a teaspoon or palette knife to create some texture and height around the top and sides.
5. Bake the pavlova for 1½ hours, then turn off the oven and leave the pavlova to cool inside for an hour.
6. To serve, whisk the cream in a large bowl until it is just holding its shape. In a second bowl, briefly whisk the yogurt with the honey to loosen – no need to clean the whisk in between. Fold the yogurt into the cream to lighten it.
7. Slice the peaches and roughly chop the pistachios. Put the pavlova onto a serving plate, pile on the yogurt cream, then top with the sliced peaches and pistachios, and drizzle over the honey. An absolute winner.

Freezer Cookies

Freezer cookies have become a staple in our flat. Warning: once you start having cookies on demand, you can't go back. For this book, I wanted to perfect the recipe, and found that melted butter gives the best crunchy-on-the-outside, soft-in-the-middle texture.

Makes 12

Takes 20 minutes to make, plus 15 minutes to cut and bake whenever you like

V

125g (4½oz) salted butter

150g (5½oz) chocolate/mix-ins (use whatever you like, including your favourite chocolate bar, or maybe even some pretzels, peanuts or stem ginger)

75g (1¾oz) soft brown sugar

75g (1¾oz) caster (superfine) sugar

1 medium egg

1 teaspoon vanilla extract

175g (6oz) plain (all-purpose) flour

½ teaspoon baking powder

½ teaspoon fine salt (optional but delicious!)

*

Tips: For double-chocolate cookies, use 150g (5½oz) plain (all-purpose) flour and 25g (1oz) cocoa powder.

If you want to eat the cookies the same day, simply put the bowl of dough into the fridge to cool for a couple of hours, then ball the cookies and bake straight away.

1. Melt the butter in a saucepan over a medium heat, then leave to cool for at least 5 minutes.
2. Meanwhile, roughly chop any large pieces of chocolate and mix-ins, then set aside.
3. Pour the cooled melted butter into a large mixing bowl. Add the sugars and stir with a wooden spoon to combine. Crack in the egg, then add the vanilla extract and beat until smooth.
4. Add the flour, baking powder and salt, if using. Beat well until a smooth cookie dough forms, then stir through your chocolate/mix-ins.
5. Take a large sheet of baking paper and dollop the cookie dough into the centre, then use the baking paper to wrap the dough and shape it into a log around 7cm (2¾ inch) in diameter. I then use elastic bands to keep the paper in place at the ends, or if you prefer, you can wrap it in clingfilm. Put the cookie dough into your freezer. It can happily stay there for up to 3 months. (Alternatively, you can shape the dough into 12 golf-ball-sized cookies, or use an ice-cream scoop, and freeze them on a tray, then transfer to a plastic bag once frozen.)
6. When you want to eat a cookie, preheat your oven to 180°C/160°C fan/350°F/gas mark 4 and line a baking tray with baking paper.
7. Unwrap part of the frozen cookie-dough log and, using a serrated knife, slice off as many cookies as you like (each cookie slice should be about 2cm/¾ inch thick). Place on the prepared tray, leaving enough room for them to spread.
8. Bake for 10–12 minutes until the edges are set but the centre is still soft. Leave to cool for as long as your patience can hack it and enjoy. Life-changing.

Chocolate, Raspberry & Almond Torte

You know those chocolate tortes you get at restaurants that are so light, with a mousse-like centre, that you could happily demolish three slices... well, this is that. It took a few rounds of testing to get there, but this torte is now my failsafe having-people-round-to-dinner dessert.

Serves 10–12   Takes 55 minutes   V/GF

200g (7oz) salted butter, plus a little for greasing

2 tablespoons cocoa powder, plus extra for dusting

200g (7oz) dark chocolate

6 medium eggs

150g (5½oz) caster (superfine) sugar

50g (1¾oz) ground almonds

fine sea salt

150g (5½oz) raspberries

crème fraîche or yogurt, to serve

1. Preheat your oven to 160°C/140°C fan/325°F/gas mark 3. Grease the base and sides of a 23cm (9 inch) springform cake tin with a little butter, then dust a thin layer of cocoa powder across the base.
2. Put the butter into a heatproof bowl and snap in the dark chocolate. Melt together using the microwave on high, melting and stirring in 30-second bursts, or set it over a pan of just simmering water and stir to melt. Leave to cool slightly.
3. Separate the egg whites and yolks into two large bowls.
4. Add 75g (2¾oz) of the sugar to the egg whites and 75g (2¾oz) to the egg yolks, then, using electric beaters, whisk the egg whites until they are super white, fluffy and holding their shape.
5. Without cleaning the beaters (no need for extra washing-up!) whisk the egg yolks with their sugar until doubled in volume. Add the melted chocolate and butter to the egg-yolk mixture, along with the 2 tablespoons cocoa powder, the ground almonds and a big pinch of sea salt. Whisk briefly to combine.
6. Using a metal spoon, fold the egg whites into the egg-yolk mixture – start by adding a small spoonful to loosen the mixture and then fold in the rest, taking care to keep as much air as possible.
7. Gently spoon half the batter into the cake tin, then scatter over half the raspberries. Top with the remaining batter, and dot in the rest of the raspberries.
8. Bake for 30–35 minutes until the top of the torte is risen and the sides are set but the centre still has a noticeable wobble.
9. Leave to cool in its tin. It will sink a bit as it cools – don't worry. Slice, then serve with a big dollop of crème fraîche or yogurt. Dreamy.

*
Tip: The torte will keep happily for 3 days at room temperature in an airtight container (to keep its mousse-like texture, don't chill it).

Cardamom Crème Brûlée
with Rhubarb + Shortbread

① Cardamom Crème Brûlée

Crème brûlée is an old-school sweet that just hits the spot. When the texture is light, creamy and melt-in-the-mouth, you just can't beat it. I've spent many years perfecting this one, and love serving it as a show-off dessert with the Roasted Rhubarb (page 172) and Shortbread (opposite). This is best made with a blowtorch, but if you don't have one, don't worry – I've included grilling instructions too.

Serves 6 | Takes 1 hour 5 minutes, plus cooling | V/GF

16–20 cardamom pods or 2 teaspoons ground cardamom (what a win if you can get it ground!)

75g (2¾oz) + 6 tablespoons caster (superfine) sugar

450ml (16fl oz) double (heavy) cream

150ml (5fl oz) whole milk

½ teaspoon vanilla extract (optional – I love the sweetness it brings)

6 egg yolks (save the whites for Pops's Seeded Granola on page 197)

fine sea salt

1. Preheat your oven to 140°C/120°C fan/275°F/gas mark 1.
2. Open the cardamom pods to remove their seeds, then crush the seeds in a pestle and mortar and stir in the 75g (2¾oz) sugar. Alternatively, measure the 75g (2¾oz) sugar into a spice grinder, add the cardamom seeds, and blitz to combine. If you're able to get ground cardamom, just mix the sugar and cardamom together. Set aside.
3. Combine the cream, milk and vanilla, if using, in a saucepan over a medium heat. Heat until just steaming, stirring occasionally.
4. Meanwhile, whisk the egg yolks, cardamom sugar and a pinch of salt together in a large bowl. Gradually, while still whisking, pour in the hot cream to create a custard. Once fully combined, tip the custard into a jug – this makes it way easier to fill the ramekins.
5. Divide the custard between 6 ramekins, then carefully place them inside a large, deep roasting tin. Pour hand-hot water into the tin around the ramekins, until it comes halfway up the outside of ramekins – be careful not to pour any water into the custard itself. If it's easier to use 2 smaller roasting tins, do this instead.
6. Carefully put the crème brûlées into the oven. Bake for 40–45 minutes until the outsides are set but the centres still have a noticeable wobble.

7. Remove the ramekins from the water once they're not too hot to touch and cool for 15 minutes (on a wire rack if you have one, but don't fret if not). Transfer to the fridge, and leave to chill, uncovered, for at least 4 hours, preferably overnight.

8. When ready to serve, take the crème brûlée out of the fridge and spoon the 6 tablespoons of sugar over the top, 1 tablespoon onto each crème brûlée. Then, using a blowtorch, caramelise the top. If you don't have a blowtorch, you can slide the crème brûlée under a super-hot grill – you'll need to watch them like a hawk so that the sugar doesn't burn.

② Shortbread

Shortbread will forever remind me of my grandma, Janet, who is the reason I love baking. I've kept things simple here with a classic recipe, so please feel free to make your own variations; some chopped pistachios or vanilla would be nice.

Makes 12   Takes 20 minutes, plus cooling   V

150g (5½oz) salted butter

225g (8oz) plain (all-purpose) flour

sea salt

75g (2¾oz) caster (superfine) sugar

icing (confectioners') sugar, for dusting

1. Cut the butter into cubes. Put into a large bowl, along with the flour and a big pinch of salt.

2. Rub the butter into the flour using your fingers until it resembles sand, then stir in the caster sugar. Bring the mixture together with your hands until you have a soft dough – don't worry if it is a little crumbly, this is what makes it super buttery and short.

3. Transfer the dough onto a sheet of baking paper and use the paper to shape the dough into a rough log, around 5–6cm (2–2¼ inch) in diameter. Cool for 20 minutes.

4. Once ready to bake, cut into 12 rounds. Spread between two baking trays lined with baking paper, and bake at 180°C/160°C fan/350°F/gas mark 4 for 8–10 minutes until lightly golden. Leave to cool and dust with a little icing sugar before serving.

③ Roasted Rhubarb

Once, when I had very green rhubarb, a chef friend of mine suggested adding a few dried hibiscus flowers into the tin while roasting. The result? The pinkest rhubarb you've ever seen! It's a great hack for when the rhubarb isn't looking it's pinky best.

Serves 6 | Takes 40 minutes | V/VG/DF/GF

400g (14oz) rhubarb

juice of 1 orange

1–2 tablespoons caster (superfine) sugar

dried hibiscus flowers (optional)

*
Tip: Best made the day before for ultimate pinkness.

1. Cut the rhubarb into roughly 5cm (2 inch) batons.
2. Arrange the rhubarb in a roughly single layer in a roasting tin, then pour over the orange juice and sprinkle over the caster sugar. Scatter over a few of the dried hibiscus flowers, if using.
3. Cover the tin tightly in foil. Roast at 180°C/160°C fan/350°F/gas mark 4 for 20–30 minutes (depending on thickness) until the rhubarb is just soft – it will continue cooking as it cools. Remove the hibiscus before serving.

Richard's Ruin

This is less of a recipe, more of a dessert hack for life. All credit goes to the landlord of the first pub I worked in, part-time as a pot-washer, when I was 14. Game-changer.

Serves 2 (easily halved or doubled!)

Takes 5 minutes　　　　　　　　　　　　　　　V

4 large scoops of vanilla ice cream (get your favourite kind)

2 x 37g (1¼oz) bags of chocolate malt balls (I like Maltesers)

50–100ml (1¼–3½fl oz) Irish cream liqueur (I like Baileys), depending on how boozy you like it – for me, it's always 100ml!

1. Take your ice cream out of the freezer a good 10 minutes before you want to eat, so it can soften.
2. Using a rolling pin, lightly crush the chocolate malt balls, still in their bags.
3. Put 2 large scoops of ice cream into each bowl. Pour half the Irish cream liqueur over each, then top with the crushed chocolate malt balls. Sink into the sofa; revel.

Prune Sticky Toffee

This recipe came about by accident; I didn't have any dates, so I swapped them out for prunes instead. The result was better than the original. Baking in a loaf tin then slicing and reheating in sauce gives the best sauce-to-sponge ratio; shout-out to my girl Ells for this revelation.

Serves 8 Takes 1 hour 20 minutes V

75g (2¾oz) salted butter, plus a little extra for greasing

175g (6oz) prunes (de-stoned weight)

150ml (5fl oz) boiling water

1 teaspoon bicarbonate of soda (baking soda)

150g (5½oz) soft light brown sugar

2 medium eggs

2 tablespoons black treacle

150g (5½oz) self-raising flour

ice cream, cream or custard, to serve

fine sea salt

FOR THE SAUCE

170g (5¾oz) salted butter

170g (5¾oz) soft light brown sugar

2 heaped tablespoons black treacle

300ml (10½fl oz) double (heavy) cream

1 teaspoon vanilla extract

1. Preheat your oven to 180°C/160°C fan/350°F/gas mark 4. Grease and line a 900g (2lb) loaf tin.
2. De-stone the prunes, then blitz in a food processor to a rough paste, or chop by hand. Add to a bowl, then pour in the boiling water and the bicarb. Stir, then set aside.
3. Measure the butter and sugar into a large bowl. Whisk together (a hand whisk is fine) until well combined, then crack in the eggs and whisk again. Add the treacle, followed by the flour and a big pinch of salt. Whisk until you have a smooth batter, then add the prunes, along with their soaking liquid, and whisk again.
4. Scrape the batter into the tin. Bake for 40–45 minutes until a skewer, or piece of spaghetti, poked into the centre comes out clean. Leave to cool completely in the tin.
5. Meanwhile, make the sauce. Combine all the ingredients in a saucepan over a medium heat. Bubble away for 3–5 minutes until fully amalgamated into a luscious toffee sauce. Season with salt to taste for proper salted caramel vibes. Turn off the heat.
6. Just before serving, preheat your oven to 180°C/160°C fan/350°F/gas mark 4. Line a large roasting tray with foil.
7. Cut the sticky toffee loaf into 8 thick slices. Dollop a large spoonful of toffee sauce on top of each slice, pop on the tray then cover the tray with foil. Heat for 8–10 minutes until bubbling. Meanwhile, reheat any remaining toffee sauce in a pan to pour over. Serve each slice covered in sauce, with ice cream, cream or custard: your choice.

*

Tip: This sticky toffee loaf will taste even better the next day (it keeps for a week). Once baked and cooled, wrap it tightly in clingfilm and keep at room temperature. The sauce can be made in advance and kept in the fridge. It will harden once cold, but will come back together once reheated.

Tiramisu

I perfected my tiramisu recipe for the monthly supper club I run with my husband, Adam. One of the guests said he bought a ticket based on the fact we'd simply written 'tiramisu' for the dessert – no adaptations, and, in his opinion, boldly simple. So he thought it must be good. It's pretty damn nice.

Serves 4

Takes 30 minutes   V

200ml (7fl oz) strong coffee (use decaf if you like!)

100ml (3½fl oz) Kahlúa or rum

4 medium eggs

100g (3½oz) caster (superfine) sugar

250g (9oz) mascarpone

1 teaspoon vanilla extract

175g (6oz) sponge fingers

1 tablespoon cocoa powder

1. Make your coffee and leave to cool slightly, then pour it into a shallow bowl, along with your chosen booze. Get out a small baking dish or brownie tin.
2. Separate the egg whites and yolks into two large bowls.
3. Add 50g (1¾oz) of the sugar to the egg whites and 50g (1¾oz) to the egg yolks, then, using electric beaters, whisk the egg whites until they are super white, fluffy and holding their shape.
4. Without cleaning the beaters (no need for extra washing-up!), whisk the egg yolks with their sugar until doubled in volume. Add the mascarpone and vanilla, and whisk again until smooth. Using a metal spoon, fold the egg-white mixture into the egg-yolk mixture – start by adding a small spoonful to loosen the mixture, then fold in the rest, taking care to keep as much air as possible.
5. One at a time, dunk half of the sponge fingers into the coffee/booze mixture until they are saturated and almost falling apart, but not quite. Line them up in your chosen tiramisu dish. Once you have created a tightly packed single layer, spread over half the mascarpone mixture, then repeat, soaking the remaining sponge fingers and spreading over the remaining mascarpone.
6. Dust the top of your tiramisu with the cocoa powder. Chill for at least 4 hours, or overnight, before serving.

Lemon, Yogurt & Olive Oil Cake

I first wrote this recipe to showcase my friend Zoi Baldry's olive oil, one of the products from her company Raphael's Mediterranean Deli. She very kindly said I could put it in my book. I've tweaked the recipe slightly to include a drizzle that makes it all the more lemony – I swear it's one of those cakes that keeps getting tastier!

Serves 10–12　　　　　**Takes 1 hour 10 minutes**　　　　　　　　　　**V**

250ml (9fl oz) extra virgin olive oil, plus a little extra for greasing

250g (9oz) caster (superfine) sugar

225g (8oz) plain (all-purpose) flour

½ teaspoon fine sea salt

½ teaspoon bicarbonate of soda (baking soda)

1 teaspoon baking powder

175g (6oz) full-fat Greek yogurt, plus extra to serve

zest of 3 lemons and juice of 2 (use the other in the drizzle)

3 medium eggs

sliced strawberries, to serve (optional)

FOR THE DRIZZLE

50g (1¾oz) caster (superfine) sugar

juice of 1 lemon

Tip: This is one of those cakes that keeps getting better. It will happily keep for up to a week in an airtight container.

1. Preheat your oven to 160°C/140°C fan/325°F/gas mark 3. Lightly grease a 23cm (9 inch) springform cake tin with olive oil and line the base with baking paper.
2. In a large bowl, whisk together the sugar, flour, salt, bicarb and baking powder.
3. Place the Greek yogurt in a separate medium bowl. Add the lemon zest and juice and whisk to combine and loosen the yogurt. Crack in the eggs, then pour in the olive oil and whisk together.
4. Pour the wet ingredients into the dry and whisk until you have a smooth cake batter. Pour into the prepared cake tin and bake in the centre of the oven for 50 minutes until the cake is risen and a skewer (or piece of spaghetti!) poked into the centre comes out clean. The top will crack a little as it cooks; this is normal, and it will settle while cooling.
5. Once the cake is nearly cooked, make the drizzle. Put the sugar into a small saucepan with 50ml (2fl oz) water. Gently cook over a low heat until the sugar has dissolved, then let it bubble away for 5 minutes until a thick syrup forms. Stir in the lemon juice.
6. Remove the cake from the oven and, using a skewer or piece of spaghetti, poke holes across the top. Pour the warm syrup over the cake and leave to absorb.
7. Leave the cake to cool in its tin. Once cool, serve with Greek yogurt. I like to eat this with some sliced strawberries, when they're in season.

Key Lime Meringue Pie

I ate a lot of key lime pie growing up, and for good reason – the combination of buttery ginger biscuits and zingy lime is unparalleled. For one of our supper clubs, I decided to put my own twist on it, adding a blowtorched meringue layer. It turned something great into something fabulous. You'll need a blowtorch and a digital thermometer for this one.

Serves 12–14

Takes 1 hour 30 minutes   V

250g (9oz) ginger biscuits (I like ginger nuts)

140g (5oz) salted butter

8 limes

6 medium eggs

2 × 397g (14oz) tins condensed milk

300g (10½oz) caster (superfine) sugar

1. Preheat your oven to 160°C/140°C fan/325°F/gas mark 3.
2. Tip the biscuits into a food processor and blitz until you have fine crumbs. Alternatively, put them into a sandwich bag and smash super well with a rolling pin.
3. Melt the butter in a pan over a medium heat, then take off the heat. Add the crushed biscuits and stir to combine. If using a food processor, you can just pour the melted butter in and pulse together. The mixture should be the texture of wet sand.
4. Tip the buttery biscuits out into a 23cm (9 inch) tart case and use your fingers to evenly line the tin with the mixture, making sure you cover the base and sides. Bake the pie crust in the oven for 10 minutes, then leave to cool slightly.
5. Meanwhile, zest and juice the limes into a bowl. Separate the egg whites and yolks. Put the egg whites into a container in the fridge for later, and put the yolks into a large bowl.
6. Using an electric whisk, whisk the egg yolks until they have lightened and thickened slightly – this will take around 2 minutes. Add your condensed milk, whisk to combine, then whisk in your lime zest and juice.
7. Scrape the lime-flavoured filling into your ginger-biscuit pie crust. Bake in the centre of the oven for 15–18 minutes until the filling is just set; if you lightly shake the tart case, the middle should have a small wobble. Leave to cool completely, then chill in the fridge for at least 3 hours, or overnight.
8. When the key lime pie is cold, it's time to make your Italian meringue. Don't be nervous, it's super simple, and it can also be done up to a few hours in advance.

9. Measure the sugar into a saucepan, along with 100ml (3½fl oz) water. Place over a super-low heat and leave the sugar to dissolve – you can use the handle of a wooden spoon to lightly aggravate the sugar with the water if some bits aren't melting. Once the sugar has dissolved, increase the heat to medium and simmer away until it reaches 115°C (239°F) on a digital thermometer.

10. At this point, using an electric whisk or a stand mixer, start whisking your egg whites – you want them to get to a foamy stage. Come back to the sugar. Once it is at 121°C (250°F) remove from the heat. While continuing to whisk your egg whites, gradually and carefully pour the hot sugar syrup into the bowl, pouring it down the side so that it becomes incorporated gradually.

11. Once all the sugar has been added, keep whisking your meringue until it has cooled to room temperature and is super glossy and white. (At this point, you can cover the meringue and put it into the fridge. Once ready to use, simply re-whisk to make it glossy again.)

12. Remove the key lime pie from its tin – I find using a palette knife or cutlery knife can help gently release the edges.

13. Put the pie onto a serving plate, then pile on the meringue. Finally, use a blowtorch (the fun bit!) to caramelise the outside and be wowed by your own success. A proper showstopper.

Key Lime Meringue Pie

↓

page 178

White Chocolate & Pretzel Blondies

This recipe, with the patient help and expertise of my great friend and exceptional baker Bella, has had many tweaks. I'm very happy to say that, because of it, this blondie BANGS. It has that slightly gooey, chewy texture we all love and want, while the brown butter and salted pretzels add nutty depth that cuts through the sweetness and makes it incredibly moreish.

Serves 12   Takes 50 minutes   V

225g (8oz) salted butter, plus a little extra for greasing

150g (5½oz) white chocolate

350g (12oz) soft light brown sugar

3 medium eggs

1 tablespoon vanilla extract

240g (8½oz) plain (all-purpose) flour

½–1 teaspoon fine sea salt (for me, the blondies can take a teaspoon of salt to balance the sweetness, but as it's down to personal preference, you do you)

50g (1¾oz) salted pretzels

1. Preheat your oven to 180°C/160°C fan/350°F/gas mark 4. Grease a 20cm (8 inch) square brownie tin with butter, then line with baking paper.
2. Melt the butter in a small saucepan over a medium heat. Once melted, keep cooking the butter, whisking occasionally, until it has browned in colour and is beginning to smell nutty. Leave to cool slightly.
3. Chop the white chocolate into random chunks.
4. Measure the sugar into a large bowl, then crack in the eggs. Add the melted (browned) butter and vanilla extract. Whisk together to combine (hand whisk is best), then add the flour and salt. Whisk again until you have a smooth, caramel-coloured batter.
5. Spread half the batter into your prepared tin, then scatter over half the chocolate and break over half the pretzels. Top with the remaining batter, chocolate and pretzels – I like to keep a few pretzels whole, because it looks cute.
6. Bake in the centre of the oven for 25–30 minutes until golden brown. You want the top to be shiny, the edges set, and for the centre to still have the slightest wobble – this is the secret to a chewy centre.
7. Leave the blondie to cool in its tin. Once cool, cut into 12 squares and feel v. smug.

*
Tip: The blondies will happily keep for up to 5 days in an airtight container – if you can resist them for that long! You can also freeze them in portions.

Miso Popcorn Cereal Squares

I'm all for fancy pastries, but often my sweet craving goes back to childhood: give me a caramel slice or a chocolate Rice-Krispie cake any day. These miso-popcorn squares are seriously addictive – and manage, thanks to the miso, to be adult enough that you can 'bake' them for your mates with kudos.

Makes 12 | **Takes 20 minutes, plus setting** | **can be V/can be GF**

400g (14oz) marshmallows (check the ingredients if you're veggie)

100g (3½oz) salted butter

2–3 tablespoons white miso

140g (5oz) cereal of your choice (I like Cheerios, Rice Krispies or Cornflakes) – choose a gluten-free cereal to make these gluten free

60g (2oz) toffee popcorn

FOR THE CHOCOLATE LAYER

150g (5½oz) dark chocolate

15g (½oz) salted butter

1. Line a 20cm (8 inch) square brownie tin with baking paper.
2. Put the marshmallows, butter and miso into a large saucepan. Gently heat, stirring, until the butter and marshmallows have melted and amalgamated.
3. Take off the heat and leave to cool for a couple of minutes – this well help the mixture thicken – then beat again. Tip in the cereal and toffee popcorn.
4. Stir well to make sure everything gets coated in the marshmallow-miso mix, then dollop into your lined tin, pressing down to smooth out the top – it will be wonderfully sticky!
5. Put into the fridge to set for at least 2 hours. If you want to speed up the process, you can whack it into the freezer.
6. Once set, cut into 12 squares. Line a baking tray with baking paper.
7. For the chocolate layer, snap the chocolate into a heatproof bowl, then add the butter and melt in the microwave on high in 30-second bursts, stirring after each addition, or set the bowl over a pan of barely simmering water, stirring until melted.
8. One by one, dip the cereal squares into the melted chocolate to coat the bottoms, then place chocolate-side down on the baking paper (don't worry, they will come off easily once set).
9. Leave to set in the fridge for an hour or so, then enjoy. Childhood nostalgia, reimagined – big YUM.

*

Tip: The cereal squares will happily keep in an airtight container in the fridge for up to a week, if they last that long...

Triple-Chocolate Brownies
↓
page 186

White Chocolate
& Pretzel Blondies

page 182

Miso Popcorn Cereal Squares

page 183

Triple-Chocolate Brownies

You can't have a book about Sundays without including a brownie – the GOAT sweet. I've kept things pretty classic here. It's squidgy, soft and packed full of chocolate. After witnessing my mate Ahmed's reaction to eating these, I reckon they're my best yet.

Serves 12

Takes 50 minutes

V

250g (9oz) salted butter

200g (7oz) dark chocolate

150g (5½oz) milk and white chocolate (go for whatever mix of different chocolate bits you like)

3 medium eggs

300g (10½oz) caster (superfine) sugar

50g (1¾oz) self-raising flour

50g (1¾oz) cocoa powder

½ teaspoon sea salt flakes, plus extra to finish (if you like)

1. Preheat your oven to 180°C/160°C fan/350°F/gas mark 4. Take a small nubbin off the butter and use it to grease a 20 × 20cm (8 × 8 inch) brownie tin, then line with baking paper.
2. Put the remaining butter into a heatproof bowl, along with the dark chocolate. Melt together using the microwave on high, melting and stirring in 30-second bursts, or place the bowl over a pan of just simmering water and stir to melt. Leave to cool slightly.
3. Meanwhile, chop any larger bits of milk and white chocolate into random chunks. Set aside.
4. Crack the eggs into a large bowl. Add the sugar, then use an electric whisk to beat together until almost doubled in size – you want it to be super light and aerated.
5. Scrape in the chocolate-and-butter mixture, then add the flour, cocoa powder and salt. Briefly whisk until you have a smooth, rich chocolate batter.
6. Spread half the batter into your prepared tin, then scatter over half the chocolate pieces. Top with the remaining batter, then poke the remaining chocolate pieces into the top.
7. Bake in the centre of the oven for 25–30 minutes until the edges are set and the centre still has a nice wobble – no one wants an overcooked brownie! Sprinkle over some more sea salt, if you like, then leave the brownie to cool. Once cool, cut into 12 squares and thank me later.

Tip: These brownies will happily keep for up to 5 days in an airtight container – if they last that long! You can also freeze them in individual portions.

Coffee, Tahini & Chocolate Profiteroles

Supermarket profiteroles are a Godwin staple, although you'd better get in quick when you have three brothers with a sweet tooth who can demolish them in seconds. So, of course, I had to have profiteroles in my book, although these are better: stuffed full of coffee crème pât, and coated in chocolate, tahini and sesame seeds. It's a longer recipe, but super easy to follow, so don't be intimidated. You'll need a large piping bag.

Serves 4–6

Takes 1 hour 30 minutes   V

80g (2¾oz) cold
salted butter

100g (3½oz) plain
(all-purpose) flour

a pinch of fine sea salt

3–4 medium eggs

300ml (10½fl oz) double
(heavy) cream

1–2 tablespoons sesame
seeds, to decorate

1. Preheat your oven to 200°C/180°C fan/400°F/gas mark 6. Line two large baking trays with baking paper.
2. Cut the butter into small cubes. Add to a saucepan, along with 200ml (7fl oz) water, and bring to the boil over a medium heat.
3. Meanwhile, sift the flour into a bowl, then add the salt. Tip all the flour into the butter mixture at once, and beat like mad with a wooden spoon to create a lump-free dough.
4. Tip the dough into a large bowl, spreading it up the sides to help it cool quicker. Leave for 5 minutes until just warm to the touch.
5. Meanwhile, crack the eggs into a jug and whisk together to combine.
6. When the dough has cooled, beat in the eggs, bit by bit, making sure each addition is incorporated before you add more. Keep adding the eggs until you have a glossy dough that reluctantly drops off the end of your spoon when you pick up a spoonful – you may not need all of the eggs to get this consistency.
7. Spoon the dough into a large piping bag, snip off the end, then pipe 40 profiteroles onto your lined baking trays, leaving a nice gap in between each one so they have room to spread. Use a wet finger to flatten any dimples on the tops of the profiteroles.
8. Bake for 20–25 minutes until the profiteroles are puffed up, crisp and deeply golden – they are ready when they come away from the paper easily.

←

FOR THE COFFEE CRÈME PÂT

400ml (14fl oz) whole milk

1 tablespoon espresso powder (use decaf if you like)

3 medium egg yolks (save the egg whites for the Peach, Honey & Yogurt Pavlova on page 164)

3 tablespoons cornflour (cornstarch)

50g (1¾oz) caster (superfine) sugar

FOR THE CHOCOLATE SAUCES

75g (2¾oz) white chocolate

75g (2¾oz) dark chocolate

2 tablespoons tahini

200ml (7fl oz) double (heavy) cream

9. Turn the profiteroles upside down and use a skewer, or the end of a teaspoon, to create a hole inside each one. Return to the oven for 5 minutes, then transfer to a wire rack to cool.

10. Coffee crème pât time. Pour the milk into a saucepan over a medium heat. Add the espresso powder and heat until just steaming.

11. Meanwhile, whisk the egg yolks, cornflour and caster sugar together in a large bowl. Gradually, while still whisking, pour in the hot milk. Once fully incorporated, pour this custard mixture back into the saucepan.

12. Cook over a medium heat, whisking, until you have a super-thick coffee custard. Transfer to a bowl, cover with clingfilm (make sure the clingfilm touches the surface of the custard to stop it getting a skin) and leave to cool completely.

13. When you're ready to eat, whisk the 300ml (10½fl oz) double cream in a bowl until it is just holding its shape. Get your cold crème pât (it will have firmed up a lot; don't worry) and whisk to loosen, then fold it into the cream. Spoon the delicious light mixture into a piping bag, then use it to fill your profiteroles.

14. For the chocolate sauces, roughly chop both the white and dark chocolate, and put them into two separate bowls. Add the tahini to the white chocolate.

15. Heat the 200ml (7fl oz) double cream in a small saucepan over a medium heat until just starting to simmer, then pour half over each bowl of chocolate. Leave to sit for 1 minute, then stir to create your chocolate sauces.

16. Decoration time. Dip 20 of the filled profiteroles into the dark chocolate sauce first, then dip the remaining 20 into the white chocolate and tahini sauce. (You want the white chocolate sauce to set a little before dipping, so do it second.) Pile them onto a platter and scatter over the sesame seeds, to serve.

*

Tip: Once cool, these profiteroles can be kept in an airtight container for up to 2 days. The crème pât can be made a couple of days in advance and kept in the fridge.

⑦

Sunday

Extras***

Crispy Bits Chilli Oil

I could legitimately put this on anything. Crispy garlic and shallots, with spiced cumin, salted peanuts and a chilli heat: it's seriously addictive. If you're allergic to peanuts, simply swap out for another salted nut instead – cashews would be delicious.

Makes around 400ml (14fl oz) | Takes 35 minutes | V/VG/DF/GF

1 tablespoon cumin seeds

2 teaspoons black peppercorns

2 banana shallots

5 fat garlic cloves

300ml (10½fl oz) vegetable, sunflower or light rapeseed oil

50g (1¾oz) salted roasted peanuts

2 tablespoons sesame seeds

3 tablespoons chilli flakes

1 teaspoon caster (superfine) sugar

sea salt

*
Tip: To sterilise a glass jar, wash well in soapy water, then place upside down on a baking tray and put into the oven at 180°C/160°C fan/350°F/gas mark 4 for 15 minutes. Leave to cool before using.

1. Toast the cumin seeds and black peppercorns in a small, dry frying pan over a medium heat until smelling amazing. Tip into a pestle and mortar, then add a big pinch of salt and roughly grind. Tip into a heatproof bowl.

2. Place a second heatproof bowl next to your stove with a metal sieve over the top. Finely slice the shallots and garlic cloves.

3. Heat the oil in the same small frying pan over a medium heat. Once visibly hot – it should be shimmering – add the shallots. Fry, stirring regularly, for around 5 minutes until evenly golden, then strain the oil and shallots through the sieve over the empty bowl. Make sure that the oil never gets too hot, or the shallots will burn. If it is a little hot, turn off the heat.

4. Tip the shallots into the bowl with the spices and carefully pour the oil back into the pan, placing it over a medium heat once more. Put the sieve back over the empty bowl.

5. Add the garlic to the oil. Fry for 1–2 minutes, stirring regularly, until very lightly golden, then strain through the sieve into the bowl as before. Tip the strained garlic into the bowl with the shallots. Leave the oil to cool for around 10–15 minutes until it is warm but not hot.

6. Meanwhile, roughly chop the peanuts. Scrape into the bowl with the shallots and garlic, along with the sesame seeds, chilli flakes and sugar. Season with a big pinch of salt, and stir together.

7. Once the oil has cooled slightly, pour it over the gubbins and give everything a good mix, then spoon into a sterilised jar. Once opened, this will keep for up to 1 month in the fridge. Use it on everything – especially the Miso Corn Rice on page 70.

Salsa Macha

Originating from Veracruz, Mexico, this salsa is a kind of hybrid between a chilli oil and a paste. I first tried it at Tacos Padre in London. Using dried chillies gives salsa macha its complex, smoky, sweet, fruity heat, while toasted seeds add body and more flavour. It's seriously addictive. Trust me, you'll end up loving this so much that your best mates will start to associate you with it (Bex!).

Makes around 600ml (21fl oz)   Takes 30 minutes, plus 30 minutes cooling   V/VG/DF/GF

6 garlic cloves

6–8 dried chillies (I like a mixture of ancho, arbol and/or habanero, but really, use whatever you can get – if you're into Mexican cooking, I recommend Cool Chile for their products)

500ml (17fl oz) light rapeseed oil or vegetable/sunflower oil

100g (3½oz) mixed seeds

1–3 teaspoons chilli flakes (depending on how spicy you want it)

2 teaspoons soft brown sugar

2 tablespoons apple cider vinegar

sea salt and freshly ground black pepper

1. Peel the garlic cloves. Remove the stalks from the dried chillies, if they have them.
2. Take out 2 heatproof bowls, and place a metal sieve over one of them.
3. Pour the oil into a small frying pan over a medium heat. Once visibly hot – it will be shimmering – add the dried chillies. Lightly fry until they puff up, then use a slotted spoon or tongs to remove them and place them in the empty bowl. You may need to do this in batches.
4. Add the garlic cloves to the oil and fry, turning regularly, until evenly golden, then transfer into the bowl with the chillies as before. Make sure that your oil never gets too hot, as you don't want to burn any of the ingredients. If it seems a little hot, just turn off the heat.
5. Next, add the mixed seeds. Fry, stirring, until they turn lightly golden (be careful, as they may pop a bit), then strain the seeds through the sieve, collecting the oil in the second bowl underneath.
6. Tip the seeds into the bowl with the chillies and garlic.
7. Leave the oil to cool for 30 minutes. Once cool, pour the oil into a food processor or blender, then add the chillies, garlic and mixed seeds, along with the chilli flakes, sugar and apple cider vinegar. Season with a good pinch of salt, then blitz until everything is very finely chopped and combined, but not completely smooth. Season the salsa to taste.
8. Pour into a sterilised glass jar (see Tip, opposite) and keep for up to 1 month. Once opened, keep in the fridge. Use on everything! I love it with my Salsa Macha Pan Con Tomate (page 32) and the fish taco feast (page 142).

Pickled Chillies

↓

page 196

**Crispy Bits
Chilli Oil**

↓

page 192

Pops's Seeded Granola
↓
page 197

Salsa Macha
↓
page 193

Pickled Chillies

These pickled chillies and garlic are sweet, sour and utterly addictive. I love spooning them over noodles, rice, broth – EVERYTHING! They're particularly good paired with the Sticky Beef Cheeks on page 80.

Makes a 250ml (9fl oz) jar   Takes 10 minutes   V/VG/DF/GF

6 fat garlic cloves

6 red chillies

150ml (5fl oz) rice vinegar

100g (3½oz) caster (superfine) sugar

sea salt

1. Finely slice the garlic and chillies. Add to a sterilised jar (see Tip on page 192).
2. Put the vinegar and caster sugar into a small saucepan, along with 50ml (2fl oz) water and a big pinch of salt. Cook over a low heat until the sugar has dissolved, then increase the heat to medium and bring to a simmer.
3. Once simmering, pour the pickling liquid over the chillies and garlic. Leave to cool completely, then keep in the fridge for up to 6 weeks.
4. The chillies are good to eat once the pickling liquor is cold, but I like to wait a day or two, so that the flavours can mellow. The longer you leave them, the sweeter and tangier they become.

Pops's Seeded Granola

This seeded cinnamon, ginger and honey granola came about because my best mate and housemate, Pops, needed a nut-free breakfast to take into work. Egg white is the secret ingredient here to give you nice big clusters. If you're vegan, feel free to leave it out and sub the honey for maple syrup instead.

Makes around 1.5kg (3lb 5oz)	Takes 45 minutes	V/DF/can be GF (check the oats)

500g (1lb 2oz) porridge oats

500g (1lb 2oz) mixed seeds (use up whatever you have – a combination of sunflower, sesame and pumpkin seeds/pepitas works well)

4 tablespoons ground cinnamon

2 tablespoons ground ginger

150g (5½oz) coconut oil

150g (5½oz) honey or maple syrup

2 egg whites (save the yolks and use them in the Roasted Garlic Veggie Caesar on page 130 or the Cardamom Crème Brûlée on page 168)

sea salt

1. Preheat your oven to 180°C/160°C fan/350°F/gas mark 4. Line your largest roasting tray (or two smaller trays) with baking paper.
2. In your largest bowl, mix together the porridge oats, seeds, cinnamon and ginger, along with a good few pinches of sea salt.
3. Melt the coconut oil in a saucepan over a low heat, then pour it into the oat mixture, along with the honey or maple syrup.
4. In a small bowl, whisk the egg whites using a fork until frothy, then pour these into the large bowl with the other ingredients. Give everything a good mix using a large metal spoon, making sure you evenly combine the wet and dry ingredients.
5. Tip out the mixture onto the lined tray and spread out into a roughly even layer. Bake for 25–30 minutes, stirring every 10 minutes (the bits at the edge will cook faster than those in the middle) until the granola is deeply toasted and your whole kitchen smells amazing.

*
Tip: The granola will keep in an airtight container for 6 weeks. I have made this with nuts as well; simply swap the seeds for chopped unroasted nuts. I have also subbed out the oats for the same amount of rice flakes and quinoa pops when making a gluten-free version.

Thanks

It's an honour to be writing acknowledgements for my own book; I wouldn't be in this position without an amazing team of people, notably mostly female badasses, behind me.

Thank you to my agent Holly, who helped me believe in myself and stopped me from thinking like a ghost writer. To my team at Murdoch, my amazing publisher Céline, editorial manager Virginia, design manager Sarah, Emily on the sick design, Tara and Bree on the edit, and Jemma and Nicola on publicity and marketing – you've all been so receptive of my ideas and it's been a dream to collaborate with such a talented bunch of women.

To my recipe testers and friends Anna L, Tom, Helena, Katie, Hannah, Em, Anna H, Bags and Guzzie – your input and taste buds have been invaluable, knowing that the recipes are failsafe for people cooking at home (I hope you've enjoyed the free dinners!).

To my UNBELIEVABLE shoot team – Charlie Phillips on the most stunning colourful props, thank you. Caitlin Isola, my photographer, this book wouldn't have been half as good without you. Thank you for being the perfectionist balance to my blasé, your eye for detail and lighting wizardry is incomparable. James, thanks for being an amazing assistant – your delightful zen energy, love of food and coffee-making knowledge was excellent.

Bells, where to start: not only are you the best food styling assistant/baking whizz a girl could ask for with impeccable music taste; you are one of my best friends and having you there with me on my first book shoot made me feel at ease. Bells is responsible for all the sweet pics in this book – hire her.

Ells, my ride or die – thank you for enthusiastically receiving each day's worth of pictures, always there for advice and encouraging me to strive for the best.

To Dad and Grandma; it's your food I hanker for whenever I miss home, and you both encouraged and inspired me to cook from a young age, even if to begin with it was at the detriment of having a clean kitchen. Without you I would never have started on this career.

Finally, and most importantly, the two people without whom, this book would not have been the same: Pops and Adam. You have both patiently and enthusiastically received minute updates about every single recipe, answered a-million-and-one questions and cooked/tasted pretty much every recipe in this book. I love you both so much.

Pops, thank you for putting up with having a weekly dinner menu dictated for you, and always cooking a recipe even after a 12-hour working day.

My husband Ad, your support, as always, was unparalleled. You have been there every step of the way, from answering hilarious late-night questions in bed 'Do you think spring onion would be good in the green dressing?' to cooking SO many recipes and working at the photography shoot with me. You are beyond incredible – I can't thank you enough.

Soph xx

Index

Published in 2023 by Murdoch Books, an imprint of Allen & Unwin

Murdoch Books Australia
Cammeraygal Country
83 Alexander Street
Crows Nest NSW 2065
Phone: +61 (0)2 8425 0100
murdochbooks.com.au
info@murdochbooks.com.au

Murdoch Books UK
Ormond House
26–27 Boswell Street
London WC1N 3JZ
Phone: +44 (0) 20 8785 5995
murdochbooks.co.uk
info@murdochbooks.co.uk

For corporate orders and custom publishing, contact our business
development team at salesenquiries@murdochbooks.com.au

Publisher: Céline Hughes
Editorial Manager: Virginia Birch
Design Manager: Sarah Odgers
Designer: Emily O'Neill
Editors: Tara O'Sullivan, Breanna Blundell
Photography and styling: Caitlin Isola
Props stylist: Charlie Phillips
Assistant food stylist: Bella Haycraft Mee
Production Director: Lou Playfair

*Murdoch Books acknowledges the Traditional
Owners of the Country on which we live and work.
We pay our respects to all Aboriginal and Torres
Strait Islander Elders, past and present.*

ISBN 978 1 92261 657 9

A catalogue record for this
book is available from the
National Library of Australia

A catalogue record for this book is available from
the British Library

Colour reproduction by Splitting Image Colour
Studio Pty Ltd, Wantirna, Victoria
Printed and bound in Italy by Elcograf S.p.A.

IMPORTANT: Those who might be at risk from
the effects of salmonella poisoning (the elderly,
pregnant women, young children and those
suffering from immune deficiency diseases)
should consult their doctor with any concerns
about eating raw eggs.

TABLESPOON MEASURES: We have used 20 ml
(4 teaspoon) tablespoon measures. If you are
using a 15 ml (3 teaspoon) tablespoon add
an extra teaspoon of the ingredient for each
tablespoon specified.

10 9 8 7 6 5 4 3 2

PEFC Certified
This product is from
sustainably managed
forests and controlled
sources
PEFC
PEFC/18-32-03   www.pefc.co.uk